MW01225789

All Towards Success And Fulfilment Of Desires

A SOLEMN PLEDGE FROM

True Tales Of

SHIRDI SAI BABA

PROF. DR. B.H. BRIZ-KISHORE, F.I.E.
Member: University Grants Commission
Chairman: National Council of Rural Institutes
Government of India

NEW DAWN

NEW DAWN
a division of Sterling Publishers (P) Ltd.
A-59 Okhla Industrial Area, Phase-II, New Delhi-110020.
Ph.: 26386165, 26387070
Fax: 91-11-26383788
E-mail : ghai@nde.vsnl.net.in; info@sterlingpublishers.com
Website: www.sterlingpublishers.com

A Solemn Pledge From True Tales of Shirdi Sai Baba

ISBN 81 207 2240 x
Reprint 2005

Published by Sterling Publishers Pvt. Ltd., New Delhi-110020.
Lasertypeset by Vikas Compographics, New Delhi-110020.

A SOLEMN PLEDGE

"I shall serve those who hear my stories and teachings and I will satisfy all their wishes. Even if my stories are merely listened to, all their diseases will be cured and I shall pull out my devotees from the jaws of impending dangers."

— *Shirdi Sai Baba**

* Baba's words to Shama (Madhavarao Deshpande) as recorded by Hemadpant.

REWARD FOR THE READER

Let this holy book be there in every house and be read daily with all devotion. The stories, parables and teachings of Sai Baba are truly wonderful. They will give peace and happiness to the people, afflicted with sorrows and heavily burdened with the miseries of this worldly existence and bestow on them knowledge and wisdom, both worldly and spiritual.

- **One who reads with concentration, a chapter a day, will be granted unbounded happiness and all dangers will be warded off.**
- **If one reads it with love and faith, and completes it within a week (*saptaha*), all his or her problems will disappear, and all desires will be fulfilled.**

Declarations by Sri Hemadpant (Sri Govindarao Raghunath Dabholkar), the original biographer of Shirdi Sai Baba.

CONTENTS

CLARION CALL

At the divine instance, Sri Hemadpant (Sri Govindarao Raghunath Dabholkar) was given the holy task of recording the life of Sai Baba of Shirdi. The well known and famous biography describes numerous instances and incidents of Baba fulfilling the wishes and desires of those who look to Him. Material prosperity, health and happiness are bestowed on all who recite the divine text. Baba always invited everyone to come and take and carry away "cart loads" of treasure from His inexhaustable treasure-house. He also used to exhort and encourage people to read the holy books for a specific period, such as for a week *(saptaha)*, to get their desires fulfilled and if necessary iterate *saptaha* reading in three or four cycles.

The present work is yet another form of demonstration in an easily comprehensible and visual format, of the narration of some of the innumerable instances of Baba fulfilling the desires and wishes of his devotees, towards material prosperity, begetting children, relief from suffering and cure of ailments, and of the requirements of an ordinary being in the modern world, besides guiding true seekers of the divine to the right path. This divine book should be in everyone's house and be used as *"parayana"* (daily recitation) for fulfilling their wishes and wants.

Baba said, "There will never be any dearth or scarcity regarding food and clothes in any devotee's home. It is My special characteristic that I always look to and provide for the welfare of those devotees who worship Me wholeheartedly, with their minds ever fixed on Me".

That was the solemn promise given by Baba during His earthly sojourn and He continues to fulfil the same even now after His *Maha Samadhi.* In His own words, He declared, "Believe Me, though I pass away, My bones in My tomb will give you hope and confidence. Not only I, but My tomb will speak, move and communicate with those who surrender themselves wholeheartedly to Me."

This book is the essence of *Sai Satcharita.* It bestows the same benefit as that of reading the original divine text. This is a comprehensive version with illustrations, suitable for seekers who find themselves caught up in earthly schedules, and who, with all devotion, can complete reading it in a short time to fulfil their needs.

Through the divine inspiration of Sai Baba himself, the illustrations could be executed by Shri Bhavaraju Satyamurthy.

Divine prompting made the writing of this holy text possible, and Baba fulfilling the prayer of the writer, and his wife, Dr (Mrs) Dasu Hymavathi, received the blessings of Baba who presented Himself in the form of a photograph, the exact picture for which they had been frantically looking for, for inclusion in this book, besides *udi*, *prasad* and sacred clothes (*Sesha Vasthrams*), specially delivered to them from Shirdi. The writer, and his wife, his son Chi. Bhargva Teja, are greatly indebted to Baba for His grace, for ever and ever.

Humble salutations to Shirdi Sai Bhagawan and to the original author for making this work possible as a ready reckoner for His innumerable children.

Plot No 809
Road No. 41
Jubilee Hills
Hyderabad-500033

— Prof. Dr B. H. Briz-Kishore
October 9, 1999

"Blessed is the face of Sai. If we cast a glance at Him for a moment, He destroys all the sorrows of many past births and confers great bliss on us, and if He looks at us with grace, our bondage of *Karma* is immediately snapped and we are led to total happiness."

- *Revelation to and affirmation*
by Sri Hemadpant.

Baba, the boon giver, depicted as the *Kalpavriksha* (the celestial tree), *Kamadhenu* (the celestial cow), and *Akshya-Patra* (the celestial bowl), etc.

1. DESIRE FULFILLER AND FORTUNE SPINNER

Conventional spiritual teachings say that giving up of desires is a prerequisite for the attainment of happiness and spiritual advancement, because of the belief that desires are evil and are also the root cause of unhappiness. But desires are inextricably bound to life, since a living being is subjected to the three *gunas,* which, by their very nature stimulate desires. A superficial understanding of this tenet is bound to cause confusion in a person's mind, as we know that giving up desires is almost impossible for human nature, and consequently, happiness and peace cannot be attained in one's life.

The uniqueness of Shri Shirdi Sai Baba lies in the fact that He positively assured the people going to Him that He would fulfil all their desires and wants if they cast their burdens on Him. He unhesitatingly encouraged them to come to Him with their desires, hopes and aspirations and promised to grant their wishes. He is a *Kalpavriksha* (celestial wish-fulfilling tree), and *Kamadhenu* (boon-bestowing celestial cow).

Another extraordinary aspect of Shirdi Sai is his affirmation that He will continue to be active and respond (even after leaving His earthly body) to the pleas and prayers of His devotees and take care of them from His tomb. He was a man of God, who said these things while He was alive, and who, while living, impressed everyone as an extraordinary being with a clear manifestation of superhuman qualities.

A Miracle Man controlling the natural elements and granting peace, prosperity and happiness by fulfilling all material desires.

2. THE MIRACLE MAN

Sai Baba was aware of the past, present and future, what was happening at any moment anywhere, and what thoughts were passing through the minds of people; for, after all, thoughts also have their origin in consciousness. Being in a general state of spiritual super-consciousness, Baba could make things happen at will, beyond the limitations of physical laws.

To put it in another way, the fact that Baba could, as shown by several instances given in the biography, bring about miracles, shows that He is established in a state of consciousness in which He can will anything to happen. It was natural, therefore, for Him to be present at will – physically or in some other manifestation – wherever and whenever He wanted.

The extraordinary miraculous powers of control over all natural elements (curing the sick and granting their wishes, and coming to the aid of those who prayed to him) exhibited by Shirdi Sai Baba are recorded in His life history.

Bestowing sight on the blind, children to the childless, curing even chronic patients, conferring health on the suffering, and showering happiness and prosperity — all this was done lovingly by the Baba. Satisfying the mundane demands of devotees, like getting them a job, a promotion or a house, are a few of the many things He did for His devotees.

The universality of Baba's divinity encompassing all religions and His appearance in the form of Siva, Rama, Krishna, Maruti and Dattatreya, the Indian deities.

3. UNIVERSALITY OF BABA'S DIVINITY

Baba did not belong to any particular religion or tradition of spiritual gurus, and did not advocate any particular spiritual traditions or path for His followers. He very frequently used to utter the words *"Sab ka Malik ek"*, indicating that God is one.

By His dress and frequent invocation of "ALLAH", He appeared to be a Muslim, but He Himself indicated to some of His close devotees that He was a Hindu.

He did not openly declare Himself to be a guru or spiritual preceptor, but he was *a Sadguru,* who had given evidence and was established to lead his followers to the ultimate Truth. He gave succour to His devotees by a mere glance or touch.

Sai Baba demonstrated the extraordinary universality of His divinity in another manner, by manifesting Himself to some of His devotees as their own chosen deity, e.g., Sri Rama, Krishna, Maruthi and Dattatreya.

He sought to tell His devotees that divinity was universal, although its manifestations may be different and varied.

The essence of Baba's teaching was, without doubt, based on the *vedanta* – according to which the ultimate Truth is one and universal.

The timely intervention of Baba saved Damu Anna from doing speculation business in rice and cotton.

4. BLESSING BUSINESS AND TRADE

Damu Anna, a businessman, was approached by his friends from Mumbai to speculate in cotton, which they believed would bring them a profit of two lakh rupees. Being a devotee of Baba, he wrote a letter, requesting Baba to give His advice on the matter. Without even seeing the letter, Baba said "What does he write, and what does he plan. He wants to reach the sky. He is not content with what God has given him." After Shama read the letter, Baba said that the Seth (Damu Anna) should be content with what he had.

After receiving Baba's advice, Damu Anna immediately went to Shirdi thinking that Baba would encourage him if he met Him personally. He thought that he would give a share of the profit to Baba if he helped him in the transaction. Baba read his mind and said, "Bapu, I do not want to be entangled in such worldly things (sharing profits)." So Damu Anna dropped the idea.

On yet another occasion, when Damu Anna thought of trading in grain, rice, wheat and other groceries, Baba read his mind and told him "You will be buying at five seers a rupee and selling at seven seers a rupee", meaning that it would not be profitable at that time. Due to abundant rain and abundant crops, the prices fell, and those who had stored grains suffered heavy loses.

Due to the timely advice of compassionate Baba, Damu Anna was twice saved from disaster in business.

Tendulkar being blessed by Baba to make him pass the medical examination, against astrological predictions.

5. SUCCESS IN THE MEDICAL EXAMINATION

The Tendulkar family (Mrs. Savitribai and Ragunathrao) in Bandra, a suburb of Mumbai, were devotees of Baba. When one of their sons was preparing for the medical examination, an astrologer told him that time was not in his favour at that time. This depressed the boy .

A few days later, when his mother went to Shirdi and mentioned to Baba her son's depression, Baba told her, "Tell your son to believe in Me. Ask him to put aside all horoscopes and predictions of astrologers and palmists, and to carry on with his studies. Let him appear for the examination, as per schedule, with a calm mind. He is sure to pass this year. Ask him to put all his trust in Me, and I shall not disappoint him".

On returning home, the mother conveyed Baba's assurance to the son. Hearing Baba's message, he appeared for the examination and did the written part well, but was hesitant to appear for the oral examination. However, the examiner asked him to appear as he had done well in the written examination. He appeared for the oral examination, and by Baba's grace, passed, against all astrological predictions that the stars were against him.

In yet another instance, one Mr Shavede of Mumbai passed his Law examination, solely with the blessings of Baba, even when his friends expressed their doubts about his passing and made fun of him. Not only did he pass the examination, but he became a successful lawyer later.

Cholkar offering sugar candy to Baba for making him pass the departmental examination.

6. GETTING THROUGH DEPARTMENTAL EXAMINATIONS

Once, Mr. Cholkar, a temporary employee in the civil court in Thane, while listening to devotional songs sung by Das Ganu in praise of Baba, silently prayed to Baba and vowed, saying, "Baba, I am a poor man, unable to support my family. If, by your grace, I pass my departmental examination and get a permanent post, I will come to Shirdi, fall at your feet and distribute sugar candy in your honour."

In course of time, Mr. Cholkar passed the examination and secured a permanent post. Being a poor man, with meagre earnings, he could not afford the expense of a trip to Shirdi. Therefore, he resolved to economise by not using sugar in his food. After saving some money, he visited Shirdi, had *darshan* of Baba, prostrated himself before Him, offered a coconut, and as per his vow, also distributed sugar candy and expressed his gratitude to Sai Baba.

When he, along with Bapusaheb Jog, who was his host at Shirdi, were about to leave, Baba told Jog, "Give him cups of tea fully saturated with sugar", obviously referring to the sacrifice made by His devotee in depriving himself of sugar, in order to save money and use it to go to Shirdi. Baba further said, "If you spread your palms with devotion before me, I am immediately with you day and night. Though I am here, I still know what you do beyond the seven seas. Go wherever you will, all over the wide world, I am with you."

Hearing these significant words, Mr. Cholkar was moved and fell at the feet of Lord Sai Baba.

Baba demanding *dakshina* from a Goan gentleman, but refusing the same voluntarily offered by the other.

7. GOAN GENTLEMEN AND THEIR VOWS

Once two gentlemen from Goa came to Shirdi for a *darshan* of Baba, and prostrated themselves before Him. Baba asked for Rs. 15/- as *dakshina* from one of them, but to the astonishment of all, refused to accept Rs.35/- which was voluntarily offered by the other. When Shama, who was present there, asked Baba about this discrimination, He replied, "Shama, you know nothing. I do not take anything from anyone. The Masjid Mayi (the mother of the mosque) calls for the redemption of debt, and the debtor pays it and he is freed."

One of them said that he had taken a vow that if he got a job he would give his first salary to God, and in course of time, he got a job with a salary of Rs. 15/- per month. Later, he got several promotions and prospered. He, however, forgot completely about his vow.

In the second story, a cook working in the other gentleman's house, robbed him of his entire savings of Rs. 30,000. When he was depressed and dejected, and was crying, *a Fakir* advised him to take a vow that until he got back his money he would give up eating one of his favourite food items, and he would visit Shirdi. He vowed only about giving up eating rice, but did not offer any money. Within fifteen days of this, the cook who had stolen the money returned it and tendered an apology to him. The second gentleman also forgot completely about the vow. But Baba appeared in his dream and reminded him about fulfilling his vow of visiting Shirdi. Therefore, Baba did not accept *dakshina* from him.

For the safe delivery of Maintai, Nanasaheb Chandorkar's daughter, Baba manifesting Himself as a *tangawala*.

8. SAFE DELIVERY

Smt. Maintai, was the daughter of Nanasaheb Chandorkar, an ardent devotee of Baba. He was the Mamlatdar at Jamner, in Khandesh district. Jamner was over 100 miles away from Shirdi. Maintai was in an advanced stage of pregnancy, and was undergoing pain and major difficulty. Nanasaheb prayed to Baba for help.

At Shirdi, at about the same time, one Mr. Ramgirbuva was planning to go to his home in Khandesh. Baba called him and asked him to go to Jamner immediately and hand over *Udi* and *Aarti* (prayer song) to Nanasaheb, and only then proceed to his home. Ramgirbuva left Shirdi and proceeded to Jamner. With the little money that he had he reached Jalgaon by train, but Jamner was still 30 miles away.

As soon as he reached Jalgaon station, a peon with a *tanga* (horse drawn carriage) was waiting for him. He travelled in the tanga to Jamner and went to the house of Nanasaheb, and as instructed by Baba, delivered *Udi* and *Aarti*. Immediately, the holy *Udi* was mixed in water and was given to Maintai to drink, and *arti* was sung. After a few minutes, she had a safe delivery.

While taking leave, Ramgirbuva profusely thanked Nanasaheb for sending the peon with the *tanga* to the station to receive him. The latter was surprised, and said that he had not sent any *tanga* or peon, and he had not been aware of anyone coming from Shirdi. Ramgirbuva immediately rushed out of the house and found that there was no *tanga* or peon. These incidents reveal Baba's response to His devotees' pleas.

Baba's prior information of the arrival of Nanasaheb Chandorkar to Shirdi and his sudden transfer to Pandharpur.

9. THE SAINT — THE CLAIRVOYANT

Sri Nanasaheb Chandorkar, a Mamlatdar of Nandurbar, in Khandesh, was suddenly transfered to Pandharpur, a holy temple town of lord *Vithoba.* He was an ardent devotee of Baba. As he had to take immediate charge, he left without informing anybody. He wanted to proceed first to Shirdi to get the blessings of Baba before going to Pandharpur to take charge of his post.

At Shirdi, no one knew that Nanasaheb was on his way to Pandharpur via Shirdi. However, the omniscient Baba was aware of every movement of his devotees. When Nanasaheb approached Neemgaon, a village a few miles away from Shirdi, Baba, who was in the Masjid and talking with Mhalaspathi, Appa Shinde and Kashiram, suddenly said "Let all four of us do some *Bhajan.* The doors of Pandhari are open. Let us all merrily sing", and started singing in chrous, "I have to go to Pandharpur, and I have to stay on there, for it is the house of My Lord" — that was the gist of the song.

In a short while, Nanasaheb arrived with his family, prostrated himself before Baba, and prayed to Him to accompany them to Pandharpur and stay with them. Fellow devotees told Nana that Baba was already in the mood of going to Pandharpur and staying there. On hearing this, Nana fell at the Holy feet of Baba, with a heart filled with gratitude for knowing his inner feelings and thoughts.

Baba advising Shama to accompany Mirikar to Chitali to protect him from snake bite.

10. MIRIKAR AND THE SNAKE

Babasaheb Mirikar, the Mamlatdar of Kopergaon, on his tour to Chitali, came to Shirdi for *darshan* of Baba, and prostrated himself at His feet. Baba, while enquiring about his health and welfare, said "Do you know about our *Dwaraka Mai*. This is our *Dwaraka Mai* where you are sitting now. She wards off all dangers and anxieties of her children who sit on her lap. This *Masjid Mai* is very merciful. She is the mother of simple devotees whom she saves from calamities. Once a person sits here, all his troubles are over for ever. He who rests in Her shade attains bliss." Saying these words, Baba gave Holy ash (*Udi*) to Mirikar and blessed him. When Mirikar was about to leave, Baba again said, gesturing with his hand like a snake, "Do you know this *Lamba Bava* (tall gentlemen). He is so terrible, but what can he do to the children of *Dwaraka Mai*. When *Dwaraka Mai* protects, what can serpents do?"

Everyone was puzzled, but no one asked Him what He meant. On Baba's instructions, Shama accompanied Mirikar to Chitali. They reached Chitali by 9 p.m. and halted at the Maruthi temple. While Mirikar was sitting, engrossed in reading a newspaper, a snake was slowly moving about on his upper garment, making a rustling noise. The peon, who was nearby, saw the snake and raised an alarm. Mirikar was very frightened. Shama was also shocked. In the meanwhile, the serpent slowly climbed down from Mirikar's waist and was killed immediately. Mirikar was thus saved by the blessings of Baba.

Childless Ruttonji Wadia being blessed with a son by Baba.

11. CHILDREN TO THE CHILDLESS

Ruttonji Shapurji Wadia, a Parsi mill contractor, lived in Nanded, in the erstwhile Nizam's state. He was a rich and prosperous man, possessing enormous wealth and property. Although he appeared to be happy, he was unhappy and miserable within, as he did not have any children. One day, on the advice of Das Ganu, an ardent devotee of Sai Baba, he went to Shirdi for *darshan* and the blessing of Baba.

Ruttonji had *darshan* of Baba and offered flowers and fruits. He fell at His feet and prayed for a son, saying, "Many persons who find themselves in difficult situations come to you and you relieve them immediately. Hearing this, I have anxiously sought your feet. Please do not disappoint me." Moved by his devotion, Baba told him that his bad days were over, and giving him *Udi,* placed His Divine hand on Ruttonji's head, and blessed him, saying *Allah* (God) would fullfil his desire. Thus blessed by Baba, Ruttonji returned to Nanded, and in due course, was blessed with a son, and later had several children.

Similarly, Baba also blessed Mrs. Aurangabadkar, a lady from Sholapur, who was childless for 27 years. Mrs. Aurangabadkar, the wife of Shakharam Aurangabadkar, came to Shirdi as a last resort, to pray to Baba for a child. When she bowed and presented a coconut to Baba, Shama prayed to Baba on her behalf. Baba blessed her and said, "She will have a child in twelve months". According to Baba's word, she delivered a son in one year's time.

Damu Anna being blessed with several children through the miracle of mangoes.

12. MANGOES AND MOTHERHOOD

Businessman Damu Anna had two wives, but he did not have any children. As per the astrologer's predictions, there was no prospect of his having any children at all in his life, since there was a *papi* (inauspicious) planet in his horoscope.

One day, Baba received a parcel of 300 good mangoes, sent by a devotee from Goa. After opening it, He handed all the mangoes to Shama, except four, which He retained and put in a tin pot *(Kolomba),* saying "These four fruits are for Damu Anna".

Two hours later, Damu Anna reached Shirdi and came to Sai Baba. Baba said, "Though others want these mangoes, they are Damayya's (Damu Anna's). He, to whom these mangoes belong, should eat and die". On hearing these words, Damu Anna was shocked and frightened, but the explanation and the interpretation of *Mhalsapathi* (the priest of Khandoba temple), actually meant the death of one's ego, through surrendering one's self at the feet of Baba, and the words of Baba which were a blessing for him, satisfied him, and he said that he would accept the fruits and eat them. Baba then intervened, and told him "Do not eat them yourself. Give them to your junior wife. This *Amra Leela* (miracle of mangoes) will bear her four sons and four daughters". Damu Anna followed this command, and in due course Baba's words of blessings turned out to be true against all the astrological predictions.

Baba spotting Chand Patil's lost horse after two long months of diligent and vain search by Chand Patil.

13. SPOTTING THE LOST HORSE

Chand Patil, a Mohammadan gentlemen from the village Dhoop of Aurangabad district in the Nizam's state, lost his pet horse of whom he was very fond, while making a trip to Aurangabad. After a diligent search in vain for two long months, he was returning home, carrying the redundant saddle on his back. He found a queer fellow with a cap on his head, a long robe *(kafni),* and a short stick *(satka)* under His arm, sitting under a mango tree. On seeing Chand Patil pass by, Baba, who was sitting under the tree preparing a smoking pipe (*chillum*), called him and asked him to smoke the *chillum* and take some rest. When Chand Patil told Baba about his lost horse, Baba advised him to look for it near a *nala* (stream). Chand Patil searched accordingly, and to his pleasant surprise, he found his horse and returned happily to Baba with it.

Then Baba provided the items required for making the *chillum* miraculously in the following way. He thrust the steel prong *(satka)* forcibly into the ground and pulled out a burning charcoal. He again thrust his *satka* into the ground, and immediately water began to flow out. He put the burning charcoal in the *chillum* and wet it with this water and started to smoke, and also asked Patil to join him.

On seeing this miraculous performance of creating fire and water, Chand Patil was spellbound and realised that Baba was not an ordinary man, but an *Avalia* (a great saint) who had immense control over the five elements of nature.

Baba destroying evil astrological predictions and saving Bapusaheb Booty from a snake bite.

14. A FAVOUR — AGAINST ASTROLOGICAL PREDICTIONS

One day at Shirdi, Nanasaheb Dengale, a great astrologer, told Bapusaheb Booty, "Today is an inauspicious day for you. There is a danger to your life". Hearing this Bapusaheb Booty was greatly disturbed and became restless.

When both of them came to the Masjid, Baba asked Bapusaheb, "What does this Nana say? He foretells death for you. Well, you need not be afraid. Tell him boldly — let us see how death kills when I am here".

However, in the evening, when Bapusaheb, along with the servant, went out into the fields to ease himself, he saw a snake near him. Though he was very frightened, he remained calm.

When the servant saw the snake, he immediately picked up a stone to kill it. Bapusaheb advised him to go and get a big stick.

Before the servant came with the stick, the snake quickly moved away and disappeared into the field. Bapusaheb remembered, with joy and gratitude, Baba's words of fearlessness.

Baba's foresight and protective blessings saved Bapusaheb, averting the danger predicted by the astrologer.

The benevolent Baba thus protects his devotees from harm.

Baba stalling the spreading of snake poison from Shama's little finger by preventing him from climbing the steps, and by uttering the words, "Go", "Get away", "Come down".

15. SAVING FROM SNAKE BITE

Once Shama was bitten by a poisonous snake on his little finger. The pain was severe and the poison was spreading in his body, and he feared that he would soon die. He ran to the Masjid to pray to Baba, and was about to climb the steps of the Masjid. But on seeing Shama, Baba angrily shouted at him saying, "Oh vile priest, do not climb up. Beware if you do so." And then He got enraged and roared the words, "Go ! Get away ! Come down!".

On seeing Baba's anger directed at him, Shama was dismayed and disappointed and wondered where else to go, when the God he believed to be his sole refuge drove him away. He lost all hope in life and kept silent.

However, after a while, Baba's temper cooled down, and when Shama went and sat by His side, Baba consoled him and asked him to stay at home without anxiety and fear, telling him that the merciful *fakir* would save him.

The words of Baba, like "go", "get away" and "come down" were not addressed to Shama, as he apparently thought, but they were a direct order to the snake, so that its poison did not circulate through Shama's body. Thus, Baba saved Shama merely by His words, which acted as a *mantra* and drew out the poison. Shama recovered after sometime.

Baba pushing His hand into the fire to save the blacksmith's child, even at the cost of burning His hand.

16. PROTECTING THE BLACKSMITH'S CHILD

Once, in the year 1910, on the day before Diwali, Baba was sitting by the holy fireplace *(dhuni)* and thrusting the firewood into it, and the *dhuni* was burning bright, with rising flames.

Suddenly, instead of pushing in firewood, Baba thrust his hand fully into the *dhuni*, and consequently suffered burns upto his arm.

Noticing this, Madhavarao Deshpande (affectionately addressed by fellow devotees in Shirdi as Shama) grabbed Baba by the waist from behind, dragged him forcibly backwards, and asked, "Deva, why have you done this?"

Then Baba came to his senses and replied, "The wife of a blacksmith at a distant place was working the bellows near a furnace. When her husband called her, she got up in a hurry, and her little child, whom she was holding at her waist, fell into the furnace. Seeing that, I immediately thrust my hand into the furnace, pulled the child out of the fire, and saved it. I do not mind my arm being burnt, but I am glad I saved the child".

To render instant help, Baba rushes to His devotees, unmindful of His personal hardships.

Tatya Kote Patil not heeding Baba's words of caution and consequently meeting with an accident.

17. FOREWARNING ABOUT IMPENDING ACCIDENTS

One Tatya Kote Patil, while going to Kopergaon Bazar in his *tanga* (horse carriage), came in haste, stopped at the Masjid, paid obeisance to Baba and told Him that he was in a hurry to go to Kopergaon Bazar. Baba told him to forget about going to the Bazar in a hurry, and asked him to stop for a while and not go out of the village. Seeing Tatya Kote's anxiousness to go, Baba advised him to take Shama (Madhavarao Deshpande) along with him.

Ignoring Baba's directions, Tatya immediately drove away in the *tanga*. After travelling some distance beyond the village, one of the horses became restless, ran rashly, sprained its leg and fell down. Tatya escaped miraculously and was saved by Baba. He was reminded about Mother Sai's directions. On another occasion, while going to Kolhar village, he disregarded Baba's directions and drove in a *tanga,* which met with a similar accident.

In the same way, an European gentleman who left Shirdi without heeding the advice of Baba, that he should go the next day, met with an accident and had to be taken to Kopergaon hospital for treatment of his injuries. Such incidents became legends and people learned the lesson that those who disobeyed Baba's instructions met with accidents in one way or the other, and those who obeyed were safe and happy.

Baba's words abating the storm and floods and saving the village from their fury.

18. CONTROLLING THE FURY OF STORMS, FLOODS AND FIRE

One day Shirdi was overcast with clouds and was hit by a terrible storm, with powerful winds and lightning. The winds began to blow forcibly; the clouds thundered; and lightning flashed. In this furore, all creatures — birds, beasts and men — flocked to the Masjid for shelter and prayed to Baba.

Baba was moved with compassion and came out. Standing at the edge of the Masjid, he addressed the storm loudly in a thunderous voice, "Stop! Stop your fury and be calm". Surprisingly, in a few minutes, the rain subsided, the winds ceased to blow, and the storm was over, and people went back home pleased.

On another occasion, the fire in the *dhuni* was burning brightly, and suddenly the flames were seen rising upto the rafters above. But people in the Masjid did not have the courage to draw the attention of Baba to this danger and did not know what to do.

However, soon Baba Himself realised what was happening, took up His *satka* (a stick) and dashed it against the pillar in front of Him, saying "Get down, be calm". At each stroke of the *satka*, the flames abated and in a few minutes the fire in the *dhuni* came down to its normal level and became calm.

Thus, Baba's words were a command which controlled the natural elements, whether it was a storm or a fire.

Baba lighting the lamps with water instead of oil when it was refused by the traders.

19. LAMPS LIT WITH WATER

Sai Baba was very fond of oil lamps and illumination. He used to keep the Masjid lit up with oil lamps, collecting oil from the shops in the village, and he kept them burning the whole night. This had been going on for a long time.

One evening, the traders decided to test him, so they denied oil to Baba. They told Him that they did not have any oil with them. Unperturbed, Baba returned to the Masjid.

The traders also followed Baba to see how He would light up the Masjid that night.

Baba put the dry wicks in the earthen lamps. He then poured water into the *tumrel* (tin pot), which contained a few drops of oil, and drank it. Then He spat back the liquid into the tin pot.

He filled all the earthen lamps with this divine water and lighted them. The lamps burnt, and kept on burning the whole night, illuminating the whole area.

Seeing this wonderful *leela* (miracle), the traders realised their mistake, apologised to Baba and prayed for forgiveness.

Baba being an embodiment of divine love and compassion, pardoned them and dispelled the darkness around them, and asked them to be truthful in future.

Baba driving away the cholera, ordering the women who wanted to take away the wheat flour to sprinkle it on the village borders.

20. WHEAT FLOUR — CHOLERA CURE

Baba was in the regular habit of grinding wheat in a millstone. Some time during 1910, He spread a sack-cloth on the floor of the Masjid and started grinding wheat. On seeing Baba doing this, four ladies from the village pushed Him aside, took over the grinding and ground a lot of wheat flour.

They divided the flour into four parts and were about to go away with it, thinking that Baba had no need of this wheat flour, since He had no family.

Seeing this, Baba became angry and shouted at them saying, "Are you mad? Whose property are you looting? Have I ever borrowed from you that you take away this flour? Now do what I say. Take this flour and sprinkle it at the borders of the village." The ladies silently walked away and sprinkled the flour at the village borders as ordered by Baba.

This action of Baba appeared to be very strange and beyond the comprehension of the people around him at that moment. But His marvellous ways were understood in time by those who patiently waited (*saburi*); that it was for the ultimate good of the people.

Later, everyone realised that Baba had done this to stop the spread of cholera, which was prevalent all around at the time, into the village. From that time onwards, the cholera epidemic subsided and the people of the village were happy.

Baba relieving Dattopant from chronic stomach ache with his blessings.

21. RELIEVING CHRONIC STOMACH ACHE

Dattopant, a resident of Harda, was suffering from severe chronic stomach ache for the past fourteen years, without any relief, inspite of his undergoing various kinds of treatment.

On hearing that Sai Baba could cure any disease by a mere look, Dattopant went to Shirdi and prostrated himself at His feet.

Looking at him compassionately, Baba blessed him by keeping His divine hand on his head and giving him the holy ash *(Udi)*.

Dattopant was relieved at once of his chronic ailment with Baba's divine will. He left Shirdi with Baba's permission and blessing.

There are several instances where Baba's blessings, physically or through dreams, restored the health of several other devotees, like curing chronic stomach pain, ear pain, epilepsy, tuberculosis, etc.

The sufferings and afflictions of people are removed only by the compassionate and loving glances and blessings of divine incarnations.

Baba also used to utter, "Stay, cast off your anxiety! Your sufferings have come to an end. The *Fakir* here is very kind and He will cure all diseases and protect all with love and kindness."

Baba taking Master Khaparde's plague onto Himself to relieve the mother's agony and fear.

22. TAKING PLAGUE ONTO HIMSELF

Once Mrs. Dadasaheb Khaparde of Amaraoti came to Shirdi with her younger son for Baba's *darshan* and blessings, and stayed there for sometime.

One day, her son suddenly developed high fever, which was later diagnosed as the deadly bubonic plague.

The frightened mother rushed to the *wada*, met Baba while He was having his His evening stroll, and held His feet firmly. She informed Him in a trembling voice about her son's serious condition, and sought permission to leave Shirdi for Amraoti.

But Baba, in a kind and soft tone, told her, "The sky is beset with clouds, but they will melt and pass off soon and everything will be smooth and clear". And He lifted up His shirt *(kafni)* and showed to all those present there, four fully developed buboes on His waist, and added, saying, "See how I suffer for the sake of My devotees. Their difficulties are Mine."

The heart of the divine soul melts like soft wax or butter when esposed to the warmth of the prayers of suffering devotees.

By the grace of Baba, after a few days, the son was completely cured, and the mother was relieved of her anxiety.

Thus, Baba took on himself the plague of the boy and saved him from the deadly disease.

Pitale cured of epilepsy by the grace of Baba.

23. CURING EPILEPSY

Mr. Harischandra Pitale, a resident of Mumbai, had a son who was suffering from epilepsy. Inspite of extensive treatment, including Allopathic and Ayurvedic treatments, he could not be cured.

On learning that Sai Baba, by His mere touch and glance, cured many chronic diseases, he came to Shirdi with his wife and children, prostrated himself before Baba and prayed for his sick son.

However, to their utter shock, as soon as Baba looked at the sick child, he had a severe attack of epilepsy and fell down senseless. The parents became nervous and the mother started wailing, cursing themselves for coming to Shirdi, and even doubted Baba's power.

But Baba comforted her, saying, "Do not wail, have patience and wait for some time. Now take the boy to your lodge and he will come to his senses within half an hour." They did as directed by Baba, and found that His words came true and the boy recovered.

When the delighted and happy Pitale came to Baba, along with his wife and children, Baba smiled and said, "Have not all your thoughts, doubts and apprehensions calmed down now? *Hari* (God) will protect them, who have faith and patience".

After passing happy days in Baba's company, the Pitale family came to Masjid to take His leave, and Baba blessed them with *udi*.

Baba curing Bhimaj Patil from tuberculosis through dreams of flogging him with a stick and rolling a stone on his chest.

24. TUBERCULOSIS AND DREAM TREATMENT

Once Bhimaji Patil of Narayangaon (village) in Pune district suffered from a severe and chronic chest disease which resulted in tuberculosis. He lost all hope when he did not get any relief, even after he tried all kinds of treatments.

On the advice of Nanasaheb Chandorkar, Patil came to Baba and put all his faith at His Holy feet and prayed to Him to cure him.

Baba's heart melted and He spoke to him firmly, saying, "Stay and cast off your anxiety. Your suffering has come to an end. However oppressed and troubled one might be, as soon as he steps into the Masjid, he is on the pathway to happiness. The Saint (Fakir) here is very kind and He will cure the disease and protect all with love and kindness". The instant Baba uttered these words of hope and mercy, Bhimaji Patil's health took a favourable turn for the better.

Unexpectedly, he had two dreams. In the first dream, Patil as a young boy, suffered a severe flogging for reciting *"sawai poetry"* lessons before his class master. In the second dream, he suffered intense pain through torture inflicted on him by rolling a stone on his chest.

Through the pain and suffering he had to undergo in his dreams, Bhimaji Patil was cured completely, and he went home happily. From then on he was a grateful and regular visitor to Shirdi.

Baba averting Alandi Swamy's ear surgery, to the great astonishment of the doctors.

25. AVERTING EAR SURGERY

A *Swamy* from Alandi was in Shirdi for Baba's *darshan*. He was suffering from severe pain in the ear. Although he had been operated on by a doctor in Mumbai, he did not get any relief and was spending sleepless nights.

After staying for some time at Shirdi, when he came to Baba to take leave, Shama, a close and ardent devotee of Baba, prayed to Him to relieve Alandi Swamy of his suffering. Baba comforted him by saying, "God will make him all right *(Allah achcha karega)*".

With blessings and assurance from Baba, Alandi Swamy returned to Pune, and after some days, he wrote to Shama, saying that he was relieved of the pain by the blessings of Baba, but that there was some swelling still. He went to Mumbai to get rid of the swelling by an operation.

The surgeon, after a thorough examination, told him that everything was normal and there was no need for any operation.

Baba's words had a wonderful curative effect on Alandi Swamy and he was freed from his suffering.

Similarly, Baba cured Bala Ganpat Shimpi of malignant malaria, Bapusaheb Booty of dysentry and vomitting, Dr. Pillai of cholera, with just His words of assurance.

Das Ganu's vision of Pandharpur's Vittal at Shirdi.

26. *DARSHAN* OF GOD — REWARD OF DEVOUT FAITH

Once when Baba asked Das Ganu to conduct *nama saptaha* (chanting the names of God continuously for one week), he agreed to do so, but with a condition that at the end of the *saptaha*, Baba should make *Vittal* (one form of the deity worshipped at Pandharpur) appear (manifest Himself) before him.

Baba replied, "*Vittal* will certainly appear if one is earnest and devout. You need not go to far off places. Pandharpur of *Vittal* and Dwaraka of *Sri Krishna* are here".

After completing the *saptaha*, Das Ganu saw the vision of *Vittal* in Shirdi itself.

Kakasaheb Dikshit was sitting as usual in meditation after his bath when he saw *Vittal* in a vision. When he went at noon for Baba's darshan, Baba asked him point blank, "Did *Vittal* Patil come? Did you see Him? Catch Him firmly, otherwise He will escape. Hold Him firmly, otherwise He will run away, if you are inattentive".

Dikshit had another *darshan* of *Vittal* at noon. A hawker was selling pictures of *Vittoba*, and the pictures exactly looked like the one Kakasaheb saw in his vision. He bought a photo for worship.

In other instance, Baba gave *darshan* to Moolay Sastry as his Guru *Goraknath,* and as Lord *Rama* to a doctor.

Baba revealing to Mrs. Tarkhad that He had demanded and eaten the bread given by her, in the form of the dog.

27. MANIFESTATION THROUGH ALL BEINGS

Once Mrs. Tarkhad, after preparing food for everyone in the house, was about to serve the dishes, when she heard a hungry dog barking.

She immediately took a piece of bread and threw it to the dog, who ate it with great satisfaction.

Later, when she went to the Masjid, Baba said to her, "Mother you have fed me sumptuously. My afflicted *pranas* have been satisfied. Acts like this will stand you in good stead. Sitting in the Masjid, I never speak the untruth. First give bread to the hungry, and then eat yourself. Note this well".

Mrs. Tarkhad was puzzled and did not understand what Baba was saying. Therefore, she questioned Him, "Baba, how could I feed You when I am dependent on others and take my food as payment?"

Baba replied, "Eating that lovely bread, I am heartily content, and am still belching. The dog you saw, and to whom you gave the piece of bread is one with Me. I roam in their forms. He who sees Me in all these creatures, is My beloved. So abandon the sense of duality and distinction and serve Me as you did today".

Baba, thus explained that He was present everywhere and in everyone.

Baba attending Deo's *Udyapan* ceremony, along with two others, as promised, by presenting Himself as a *Sanyasi* at Deo's residence at Dhanu (Thane district), while He was at Shirdi.

28. PROMISE AND FULFILMENT

Mr. Deo, an ardent devotee of Baba, had requested Him, through Bapusaheb Jog, praying to Him to participate in the *udyapan* ceremony (feast). When Jog conveyed his prayer to Baba, He said " I always think of those who remember Me. I do not require any conveyance, like a *tanga*, train or an aeroplane. I run and manifest Myself to him, who lovingly calls Me. Write to him that three of us, i.e., I, you and a third one will go and attend the *udyapan*." Mr. Jog conveyed this to Mr. Deo.

In course of time, a *sanyasi* (ascetic) came to Deo and asked for charity. Deo asked him to come later. The *sanyasi* came to Deo's house again on the morning of the *udyapan* ceremony, and told him that he had come along with two lads to eat, and not for subscription, Deo welcomed him and asked him to come in. The three of them came in, took part in the feast, and left.

After the ceremony and feast was over, Deo wrote a letter to Jog, complaining that Baba had not kept His promise. When Jog told Baba about the letter, He said, "Ah ! he says I promised to come but deceived him. Inform him that I did attend the feast with two others, but he failed to recognise Me. Why did he call me at all? He mistook the *sanyasi* for someone else. Did I not tell him that I, along with two others, would go for the feast, and did not the trio eat there? To keep My promise, I shall sacrifice My life, but never will I be untrue to my word".

Baba demonstrating to a rich gentleman, who sought *Brahma Jnana* quickly, how avarice and attachment become impediments to self-realisation.

29. WAY TO *BRAHMA JNANA*

With a desire to get *Brahma Jnana* from Sai Baba, a rich gentleman went to Shirdi. After reaching Shirdi, he went straight to Baba in the Masjid, and prostrating himself before Him, said, "I have heard that you can show *Brahma* instantly, so I have come from a far off place. I am tired after my journey. If you show me *Brahma,* all my troubles and tribulations will be over, and I will be well rewarded. Please show me *Brahma".*

Immediately Baba said, "Oh my dear friend, do not be anxious, I shall show you *Brahma* immediately. My dealings are always in cash and never on credit. Many people come to me and ask for wealth, health, power, honour, position and cures for diseases and other temporal matters. Rare is the person who comes here and asks me for *Brahma Jnana* — I shall show you, with pleasure, *Brahma Jnana* with all its accompaniments and complications". Engaging him in some other talk, Baba made him forget the topic of *Brahma Jnana.*

Meanwhile, Baba sent a boy to get a loan of five rupees from a Mr. Nandu Marwari, but the house was locked, so he was sent to other places to fetch five rupees, but in vain. Although the rich gentleman had money in his pocket, he sat there without showing any reaction.

Baba then asked the gentleman to take out Rs.250/-from his pocket, i.e., fifty times Rs.5/-, the amount He had been trying to get, and to the surprise of all, the rich man had exactly Rs.250/-. Realising the omniscience of Baba, the gentleman fell at Baba's feet, who told him that unless he got rid of avarice and greed, he could not attain *Brahma Jnana.*

Baba ordering the Ganga and Yamuna rivers to be at His feet to satisfy Das Ganu's desire to have a bath in the Prayag.

30. PRAYAG AT THE HOLY FEET

Das Ganu, another ardent devotee of Baba, desired to bathe at the holy *tirth* of the Prayag, the confluence of the holy rivers, Ganga and Yamuna, in northern India.

This bath is very meritorious, and thousands of piligrims go there to have the sacred bath and wash away their sins.

When he went to Baba and asked His permission to go on the piligrimage, Baba said, "It is not necessary to go that far. Our Prayag is here. Believe me".

And when Das Ganu bowed and put his head at the holy feet of Baba, wonder of wonders, the waters of the holy Ganga and Yamuna flowed out from the toes of Baba. Everyone present there was amazed at this miracle.

Experiencing this miracle, Das Ganu was overwhelmed and choked with emotion. With tears of joy and bliss, and with an intense feeling of love, adoration and gratitude, he sang the glory and *leelas* of Baba.

People go to holy rivers like the Ganga, and bathe at special times to wash off their sins, but the holy rivers themselves appear to take refuge at the divine feet of Baba, and cleanse themselves.

Baba reminding Govind Balaram Mankar regarding the sweet sent by Mrs. Tarkhad through him, and eating it with relish.

31. DESIRES AND FULFILMENT

Mr. Govind Balaram Mankar, before going to Shirdi, went to see Mr. Tarkhad at his house. Mrs. Tarkhad gave a sweet to Govind and requested him to offer it to Baba at Shirdi.

Govind later went to Shirdi, visited Baba and had His *darshan,* but forgot to take the sweet given by Mrs. Tarkhad with him.

Baba asked him, "What did you bring for me?" Govind replied that he had not brought anything. Baba repeated the question, and Govind again replied in the negative.

Then Baba questioned him directly, "Did not the mother (Mrs. Tarkhad) give you some sweetmeat to be given to me?"

The boy then remembered everything, and begging Baba's pardon, ran to his lodge. He brought the sweet and gave it to Him.

As soon as it was given, Baba put it in His mouth and ate it with relish. Thus, Baba satisfied the sincere desire of Mrs. Tarkhad.

On another occasion, Baba accepted Mrs. Tarkhad's offering of a special brinjal curry, sent through Mrs. Purandare, by specially asking for it.

Baba informing Mrs. Tarkhad and her son, sitting at Shirdi, about His visit to their house at Bandra, and that He found nothing to eat there.

32. PRESENCE IN ABSENCE

Once Mr. Tarkhad asked his wife and son to go to Shirdi and spend a few days in the divine presence of Baba. The son was reluctant to go, as he was apprehensive whether his father would conduct the proper worship of Baba in his absence. However, after an assurance from the father that he would carry on the worship exactly as the son had been doing, both the mother and the son left for Shirdi.

After they left, Mr. Tarkhad carried on the ritualistic worship with all devotion, keeping lumps of sugar at the altar as *Naivedya.* But one day, after returning home for lunch, he asked the servant to serve the *Naivedya* or *prasad* before lunch. To his utter dismay, he was informed that no *Naivedya* had been offered to Baba that day. Praying to Baba to pardon him for this lapse, Mr. Tarkhad immediately wrote a letter to his son, informing him about what had happened.

On the same day, at Shirdi, just before the commencement of the noon *arati*, Baba specifically told Mrs. Tarkhad, "Mother! I went to your house at Bandra to eat something. I found the door locked, but somehow I went in, and to My disappointment, found nothing for me to eat, and so I returned unappeased."

After hearing this, the son realised that there must have been some lapse in the worship at home, and he immediately wrote a letter to his father, telling him about what Baba had said, and requesting him not to neglect performing the worship properly. The letters were received by them, respectively, the next day.

Baba promising that He will a give hundred times more than what he takes as *dakshina* — Ganpaṭhrao Bodas' incident.

33. HUNDREDFOLD RETURNS

It was a practice followed by many devotees to place some coins before Sai Baba when they visited Him. This is called the offering of *Dakshina.*

Baba used to demand *dakshina* from some devotees, but did not take it from others, even when they offered it to Him.

Sai Baba asked for *dakshina* only for the welfare of the devotees, and for teaching them the value of renunciation. He used to say, "Give with faith, with magnanimity and compassion, liberally and with modesty".

He used to spend a very small part of the *dakshina* on *chillum* (smoking pipe) and the *dhuni* (holy fireplace), and the rest of it He gave away to some deserving devotees.

While taking *dakshina,* Baba used to say, "I shall have to give back hundred times more than what I receive from the devotees".

Mr. Ganpatrao Bodas, a famous actor of those times, in his autobiography, narrates how Baba fulfilled this promise in his life. Once Baba persistently insisted on Mr. Bodas giving Him *dakshina* a number of times. Finally, Bodas emptied his money bag before Baba, and prostrated himself before Him.

The result of this was that later in life, Mr. Bodas never suffered for want of money, as it came to him abundantly.

Baba fulfilling His promise that He will be ever active and vigilant, even after casting away his mortal coil, by curing Mr. Narayanarao through his dream.

34. LIVING AFTER LIVING

Bhakta Narayanarao was a great devotee of Baba. During Baba's lifetime, he had the good fortune of visiting Shirdi twice and getting His *darshan*.

Baba attained *Maha Samadhi* in 1918, and within a year, Narayanarao fell sick and suffered a lot. None of the remedies administered to him gave him any relief.

After three years of Baba's passing away, Narayanarao wished to visit Shirdi, to pray there and to be relieved of his suffering, since the medicines prescribed by the doctors did not give him any relief..

But, somehow, he could not make the trip. He started meditating on Baba, day and night.

One night, Baba appeared to him in his dream, as if coming through a tunnel, and comforted him by saying, "Do not be anxious. From tomorrow you will improve, and within a week you will be on your feet".

Exactly within a week, as assured by Baba in his dream, Narayanrao recovered completely from his illness.

Even after attaining *Maha Samadhi*, Baba responded to the sincere and whole-hearted prayers of His loving devotees, and came to their rescue any time and at any place, appearing in their visions and dreams, and fulfilling their needs.

This is an unique incident that took place after Baba relinquished His mortal body.

The divine feat performed by Baba in leaving His mortal coil without any signs of life, and swinging back to life after three days.

35. RESURRECTION — FEAT OF THE DIVINE

An extraordinary aspect of Sai Baba is that He could leave and enter his mortal body at will, which is an unusual phenomenon, witnessed earlier in the case of Jesus, who was resurrected and appeared again after He was crucified.

Once Baba told Bhagat Mhalsapati on *Margashirsha Pournima* that He had decided to give up His *prana* (life soul) and go into *samadhi.* He said, "Protect My body for three days. If I return, it will be all right. If I do not, bury My body in that open land and fix two flags there as a mark". Saying this, Baba fell down and all the vital signs of life ceased.

Learning about this, the people in the village wanted to hold an inquest and bury the body of Baba. Mhalsapathi stoutly resisted and refused to do anything, and with Baba's body on his lap, he sat guard for three days.

After the third day, there were signs of life in Baba's body and He started breathing. He opened His eyes and returned to consciousness.

This incident amply proves that Baba exists beyond His existence, independent of space and time, which He is still proving by his appearance after his *maha samadhi.* He had declared that "he who loves Me most sees Me."

Baba going ahead of Shama at Gaya, and fulfilling His promise, by appearing through a portrait at the priest's residence.

36. AHEAD OF HIS DEVOTEES — THE GAYA TRIP

Once Mr. Kakasaheb Dixit came to Shirdi and invited Baba to attend the *Upanayanam* ceremony of his son at Nagpur. At the same time, Mr. Nanasaheb Chandorkar invited Baba to attend the wedding of his son at Gwalior. Baba asked both of them to accept Shama as His representative. Then, when both of them prayed and insisted that He should attend the functions Himself, Baba told them, "After we go to Banaras and Prayag, We shall be ahead of Shama."

Later, Shama took Baba's permission, and along with Appa Kote, went on a piligrimage to Kashi (Banaras), Prayag and Gaya, after attending the functions at Nagpur and Gwalior. After visiting Kashi and Prayag, the priest at Gaya, who arranged tours for the pilgrims, took them to his house and provided them with comfortable accommodation. To the pleasant surprise of Shama, the first thing he saw was a big portrait of Baba, which was hanging on the wall in the central part of the house where he was staying. After looking at the benevolent portrait of Baba, Shama was choked with emotion, tears of joy and gratitude welled up in his eyes, and he remembered the prophetic promise of Baba, that "after going to Banaras and Prayag, we shall be ahead of Shama."

The surprise was that this portrait of Baba had been given by Shama to the priest and the host, when the latter had visited Shirdi twelve years earlier.

CONTINUING SERVICE OF THE DIVINE

While most of the religions of the world advocate an impractical dogma,"end your desires if you wish to pursue divinity", Shirdi Sai, in complete contrast, told his devotees, "Come to Me with all your desires, for fulfilment of all your wants, by transferring your burden onto Me. I will bear them and relieve you from them at once." Shirdi Sai Baba, or "The God who physically walked the earth", solemnly promised His devotees happiness, success and material prosperity. He is unique among the *avatars* of the divine.

The extraordinary miraculous powers of control over all natural elements, coming to the aid of those who prayed to him, exhibited by Shirdi Sai Baba, are recorded in history. Bestowing sight on the blind, children to the childless, curing patients with chronic ailments, conferring health on the suffering, and showering happiness and prosperity by lovingly satisfying the mundane demands of His devotees, like getting them a job, a promotion, or a house — are a few of the many things He did for His devotees.

The uniqueness of Shirdi Sai Baba is His practice of multi-religious principles, of Islam, Christianity, Hinduism, and establishing the oneness of God, which aims to liberate mankind from distress and leads them to happiness.

Sai Baba gave His solemn assurance, through His eleven declarations, that He would continue to protect all His devotees, who look up to Him, and would fulfil their material needs. He further promised that He would speak, perform and respond to the needs of all His devotees, even after His death, from His tomb.

BRIEF SKETCHES OF IMPORTANT CHARACTERS

- **Alandi Swamy** : A *Swami* from Alandi, whose ear pain Baba astonishingly cured, by the grace of His words, without the necessity of resorting to any operation.
- **Aurangabadkar** (Mrs) : Wife of Sakharam Aurangabadkar, a lady from Sholapur (Maharastra), whom Baba blessed with a child, after she had no children for 27 years.
- **Bhimaji Patil** : Belonged to Narayangaon in Junnar Taluq, in Pune district, who suffered from chronic tuberculosis. Baba cured him through dreams. It was this Bhimaji Patil who started the *Sai Satya Vrata Pooja.*
- **Bapusaheb Mirikar** : Son of Kakasaheb Mirikar, was *mamlatdar* (Revenue Officer) of Kopergaon. Baba saved him from the impending danger of snake bite.
- **Bapusaheb Booty** : A millionaire from Nagpur who constructed the present *Samadhi Mandir*, where Shirdi Sai Baba's mortal remains rest.
- **Cholkar** : A poor temporary employee in the civil courts of Thane near Mumbai, who got a permanent post with Baba's grace.
- **Chand Patil** : A well-to-do Mohammedan gentleman from the village of Dhoop in Aurangabad district of the Nizam's state, who recovered his lost horse miraculously by Baba's

grace. It was with Chand Patil's marriage party that Baba entered Shirdi for the second time, and stayed there for ever.

- **Dattopant** : A gentleman from Harda town, who had suffered from stomach ache for 14 years and who sought Baba's feet as a last resort. Baba cured him with His grace.
- **Dadasaheb Khaparde** : Was the famous and richest advocate from Amaraoti. Baba cured Mrs. Khaparde's son by taking his illness (plague) onto His own body.
- **Das Ganu** : A police officer turned into an ardent devotee of Baba. A *vedantin* and a *haridas* (person who sings in praise of God), he spoke about the life, teaching, message and fame of Baba throughout the Mumbai presidency.
- **B.V. Deo** : A *mamlatdar* at Dahanu (Thana district), at whose mother's *udyapan* ceremony, Baba presented Himself by manifesting himself in the guise of a *sanyasi*.
- **Damu Anna Kasar** : A businessman from Ahmednagar who was blessed with children by Baba's grace, against all the predictions of the astrologers. Baba also saved him from serious business losses.
- **Hemadpant** : Govindrao Raghunath Dabhlokar, a government servant who retired in 1916. He is the author of the Divine Text, "*Sai Satcharita*" in Marathi, whom Baba aptly named "Hemadpant".
- **Harischandra Pitale** : A rich well-to-do gentleman from Mumbai, whose epileptic son was cured by Baba.
- **Kakasaheb Dixit** : A London-returned solicitor from Mumbai, who constructed a *wada* (living

place) in Shirdi for himself and other devotees, which later came to be known as Dixit *Wada*.

- **Moolay Sastry** : A great scholar from Nasik, to whom Baba gave *darshan* as his guru Gorakhnath.
- **Madhava Rao Deshpande** : Affectionately addressed by fellow devotees as 'Shama', who resigned his job as a school teacher at Shirdi, and dedicated himself to the service of Baba and His devotees. Baba cured Shama from snake bite.
- **Mhalsapathi** : Priest of the Kandoba Temple of Shirdi, who first called Baba *Sai,* and who had the privilege of spending most of his time with Baba.
- **Narayanarao** : After His *Maha Samadhi,* Baba cured Narayanarao's illness by appearing to him in his dreams.
- **Nanasaheb Chandorkar** : A *mamlatdar* (Revenue officer) at Jamner in Khandesh District. Baba, by means of a miracle saved Nanasaheb's pregnant daughter Maintai at the time of her delivery.
- **Nanasaheb Dengale** : A great astrologer whose prophecy about the death of Babasaheb Booty failed due to Baba's grace.
- **Ruttonji Shapurji Wadia** : A very rich prosperous mill contractor of Nanded in the erstwhile state of the Nizam, who was blessed with children, including a male child, by Baba's grace.
- **Ramgirbuva** : A gentleman from Shirdi, who experienced a miracle performed by Baba, who transported him in a *tanga* from Jalgaon to Jamner.

- **Tatyakote Patil** : Had the privilege of spending most of his life with Baba. Baba sacrified his life to save Tatyakote from the clutches of death.
- **Tarkhad and family** : Ramachandra Atmaram, alias Babasaheb Tarkhad, lived in Bandra near Mumbai. The family had several blissful experiences of Baba's grace.
- **Tendulkar** : A resident of Bandra, near Mumbai, whose son passed his medical examination with Baba's grace, against the prediction of astrologers. Mrs. Savitri Tendulkar published a Marathi book, *Sri Sainath Bhajan Mala*, describing Baba's *leelas*.

MORNING ARATI AT 5.15 A.M.
KĀKAḌ ĀRATĪ

1. Joḍūniyā kara

Joḍūniyā kara caraṇī ṭhevilā māthā,
Parisāvī vinantī māzī Sadgurunāthā. ...1
Aso-naso bhāva ālo tuziyā ṭhāyā
Kṛpādṛṣṭī pāhe majakaḍe Sadgururāyā. ...2
Akhaṅdita asāve aise vāṭate pāyī,
Sāṅḍūnī saṅkoca ṭhāva thoḍāsā deī. ...3
Tukā mhaṇe Devā māzī veḍīvākuḍī
Nāme bhavapāśa hātī āpulyā toḍī. ...4

2. Uṭhā Pāṅḍuraṅgā

Uṭhā Pāṅduraṅgā āta prabhāta samayo pātalā,
Vaiṣṇavāṅcā meḷā garuḍapārī dāṭalā. ...1
Garuḍa-pārāpāsūnī mahādvārā-prayaṅta,
Sauravarāṅcī māṅdī ubhī joḍūniyā hāta. ...2
Śuka-Sanak-ādika Nārada-Tuṁbara bhaktāṅcyā koṭī,
Triśūla ḍamarū gheuni ubhā Girijecā patī. ...3
Kalīyugicā bhakta Nāmā ubhā kīrtanī.
Pāṭhīmāge ubhī ḍoḷā lāvūniyā Janī. ...4

3. Uṭhā uṭhā

Uṭhā uṭhā Śrī Sāīnātha Guru caraṇakamala dāvā
Ādhi vyādhi bhavatāpa vārunī tārā jaḍajīvā ...dhṛ
Gelī tumhāṅ soḍuniyā bhava-tama-rajanī vilayā.
Pari hī ajñānāsī tumacī bhulavi yogamāyā.
Śakti na āmhāṅ yatkiṅcitahī tijalā sārāyā.
Tumhīca tīte sāruni dāvā mukha jana tārāyā ...cā
Bho Sāīnātha Mahārāja bhava-timira-nāśaka ravī.
Ajñānī āmhī kitī tumhīca varṇāvī thoravī.
Tī varṇitā bhāgale bahuvadani śeṣa vidhi kavī. ...cā
Sakṛpa houni mahimā tumacā tumhīca vadavāvā.
Ādhi...Uṭhā...1
Bhakta manī sadbhāva dharūni je tumhāṅ anusarale,
Dhāyāyastava te darśana tumace dvāri ubhe ṭhele.
Dhyānasthā tumhāṅsa pāhūnī mana amuce dhāle,
Pari tvadvacanāmṛta prāśāyāte ātura zāle. ...cā
Ughaḍūnī netra-kamalā dīnabaṅdhu Ramākāṅtā,
Pāhī bā kṛpādṛṣṭī bālakā jaśī mātā.
Raṅjavī madhuravāṇī harī tāpa Sāīnāṭhā ...cā
Āmhīca apule kājāstava tuja kaṣṭavito Devā.
Sahana kariśila te aikuni dyāvī bheṭa Kṛṣṇa dhāvā
uṭhā...ādhivyādhi...2

4. Daraśana dyā

Uṭhā Pāṅduraṅgā ātā daraśana dyā sakaḷā
Zālā aruṇodaya saralī nidrecī veḷā. ...1

Saṁta sādhū munī avaghe zaletī goḷā.
Soḍā śeje sukhe ātā baghu dyā mukhakamaḷā. ...2
Raṅgamaṁḍapī mahādvārī zālīse dāṭī.
Mana utāviḷa rūpa pahāvayā dṛṣṭī. ...3
Rāhī Rakhumābāi tumhāṁ yeu dyā dayā
Śeje hālavunī jāge karā Devarāyā. ...4
Garuḍa Hanumaṁta ubhe pahātī vāṭa
Svargīce suravara gheuni āle bobhāṭa. ...5
Żāle muktadvāra lābha zālā rokaḍā
Viṣṇudāsa Nāmā ubhā gheuni kākaḍā. ...6

5. Pañcāratī

Gheuniyā pañcārātī, karū Bābāṁsī āratī.
Karū Sāīsī āratī. Karū Bābāṁsī āratī. ...1
Uṭhā uṭhā ho bāṁdhava. Ovāḷū hā Rakhumādhava.
Sāī Ramādhava. Ovāḷū hā Rakhumādhava ...2
Karūniyā sthīra mana. Pāhū gaṁbhīra he dhyāna.
Sāī ce he dhyāna. Pāhū gaṁbhīra he dhyāna. ...3
Kṛṣṇanāthā Datta-Sāī. Jaḍo citta tuze pāyī.
Citta Devā pāyī. Jaḍo citta tuze pāyī. ...4

6. Cinmayarūpa

Kākaḍa āratī karīto Sāīnāṭhā Devā.
Cinmayarūpa dākhavī gheuni bālaka laghusevā. ...dhṛ
Kāma krodha mada matsara āṭuṇi kākaḍā kelā
Vairāgyāce tūpa ghāluni mī to bhijavīlā.

Sāīnātha Guru bhakti-jvalane to mī peṭavila
Tadvṛttī jāḷunī Gurune prakāśa pāḍilā
Dvaita-tamā nāsūnī miḷavī tatsvarūpī jīvā. cinmaya
...kākaḍa...cinmaya...1

Bhū-khecara vyāpūnī avaghe hṛtkamalī rāhasī
Toci Datta Deva tū Śiraḍī rāhuni pāvasī
Rāhuni yethe anyatrahī tū bhaktāṅstava dhāvasī
Nirasuniyā saṅkaṭā dāsā anubhava dāvisī
Na kaḷe tvallīlāhī koṇyā Devā vā mānavā cinmaya
...kākaḍā...cinmaya...2

Tvadyaśa duṅdubhīne sāre aṁbara he koṅdale
Saguṇa mūrtī pāhṇyā ātura jana Śiraḍi āle
Prāśunī tvad-vacanāmṛta āmuce
dehabhāna harapale
Soḍūniyā durabhimāna mānasa tvaccaraṇī vāhile
Kṛpā karūniya Sāī-māule dāsa padarī ghyāvā cinmaya
....kākaḍā...cinmaya...3

7. Paṅḍharināthā

Bhakticiyā poṭī bodha kākaḍā jyotī
Pañcaprāṇa jīve bhāve ovāḷū āratī. ...1
Ovāḷū āratī māzyā Paṅdharīnāthā, māzyā Sāīnāthā
Donhī kara joḍonī caraṇī ṭhevilā māthā ...dhṛ
Kāya mahimā varṇū ātā sāṅgaṇe kitī
Koṭī brahmahatyā mukha pāhatā jātī. ...2
Rāhī Rakhumābāī ubhyā doghī do bāhī
Mayūrapiccha cāmare ḍhāḷiti ṭhāyīce ṭhāyī ...3
Tukā mhaṇe dīpa gheunī unmanīta śobhā
Viṭevarī ubhā dise lāvaṇya-gābhā. ...4...Ovāḷū...

8. Uṭhā uṭhā

Uṭhā sādhusaṁta sādhā āpulāle hita
Jāīla jāīla hā naradeha maga kaiṅcā bhagavaṁta. ...1
Uṭhoniyā pahāṭe Bābā ubhā ase viṭe
Caraṇa tyāṅce gomaṭe amṛta-dṛṣṭī avalokā. ...2
Uṭhā uṭhā ho vegesī calā jāūyā rāuḷāsī
Jaḷatila pātakāṅcyā rāśī kākaḍā āratī dekhiliyā ...3
Jāge karā Rukmiṇīvara, Deva āhe nijasurāta
Vege liṁbaloṇa karā dṛṣṭa hoīla tayāsī ...4
Dārī vājaṁtri vājatī ḍhola damāme garjatī
Hote kākaḍā āratī māzyā Sadguruāyāṅci ...5
Siṁ vhanāda śaṅkhabherī ānaṁda hoto mahādvārī
Keśavarāja viṭevarī Nāmā caraṇa vaṁdito. ...6

Bhajana

Sāīnātha Guru Māze āī,
Majalā ṭhāva dyāvā pāyī.
Dattārāja Guru māze āī
Majalā ṭhāva dyāvā pāyī.
Śri Saccidānaṁda Sadguru Sāīnātha
Mahārāja kī Jaya.

9. Śrī Sāīnātha Prabhātāṣṭaka
(Pṛthvī)

Prabhāta samayī nabhā śubha raviprabhā fākalī
Smare Guru sadā aśā samayi tyā chale nā kalī
Mhaṇoni kara joḍūnī karu ātā Guru prārthanā
Samartha Guru Sāīnātha puravī manovāsanā. ...1

Tamā nirasi bhānu hā Guru hi nāsi ajñānatā
Paraṅtu Guruci karī na ravihī kadhī sāmyatā
Punhā timira janma ghe Guru kṛpeni ajñānatā
Samartha Guru Sāīnātha puravī manovāsanā ...2
Ravi pragaṭa hounī tvarīta ghālavī ālasā
Tasā Guruhi soḍavī sakala duṣkṛti lālasā
Haroni abhimānahī jaḍavi tatpadī bhāvanā
Samartha Guru Sāīnātha puravī manovāsanā. ...3
Gurusi upamā dise vidhi Hariharāṅci uṇī
Kuṭhoni maga yeī tī kavani yā ugī pahuṇī
Tuzīca upamā tulā baravi śobhate sajjanā
Samartha Guru Sāīnātha puravī manovāsanā. ...4
Samādhi utaroniyā Guru calā maśidikaḍe
Tvadīya vacanokti tī madhura vāriti sākaḍe
Ajātaripu Sadguro akhilapātakā bhaṅjanā
Samartha Guru Sāīnātha puravī manovāsanā. ...5
Ahā susamayāsi yā Guru uṭhoniyā baisale
Vilokuni padāśrītā tadiya āpade nāsile
Asā suhitakāri yā jagati koṇīhī anya nā
Samartha Guru Sāīnātha puravī manovāsanā. ...6
Ase bahuta śahāṇā pari na jyā Guruci kṛpā
Na tatsvāhīta tyā kaḷe karītase rīkāmyā gapā
Jarī Gurupadā dharī sudṛḍha bhaktine to manā
Samartha Guru Sāīnātha puravī manovāsanā. ...7
Guro vinaṅtī mī karī hṛdaya-maṅdirī yā basā
Samasta jaga he Guru svarupacī ṭhaso mānasā
Ghaḍo satata satkṛti matihi de jagatpāvanā
Samartha Guru Sāīnātha puravī manovāsanā. ...8

"Stragdharā"

Preme yā aṣṭakāsī paḍhuni Guruvarā prārthitī je prabhātī
Tyāṅce cittāsi deto akhila haruniyā bhrāṅti mī nitya śāṅtī
Aise he Sāīnāthe kathuni sucavile jevi yā bālakāsi
Tevī tyā Kṛṣṇapāyī namunī savinaye arpito aṣṭakāsī ...9
Śrī Saccidānaṅda Sadguru Sāīnātha Mahārāja kī Jaya.

10. Rahama najara

Sāī rahama najara karanā,
Bacconkā pālana karanā ...dhṛ...× 2
Jānā tumane jagatpasārā,
Sabahī zūṭha jamānā ...× 2...Sāī...Sāī...1
Maiṅ aṅdhā hūṅ baṅdā āpakā,
Muzako Prabhu dikhalānā ...× 2...Sāī...2
Dāsa Gaṇū kahe aba kyā bolū,
Thaka gaī merī rasanā...× 2...Sāī...3

11. Rahama najara

Rahama najara karo, aba more Sāī,
Tuma bina nāhī muze mā-bāpa-bhaī.
Rahama najara karo, ...dhṛ...×2
Maiṅ aṅdhā hun baṅda tumhārā ...×2
Maiṅ nā jānūṅ, ...×3...allā-īlāhī...Rahama...1
Khālī jamānā maiṅ ne gamāyā, ...×2
Sāthī ākharakā ...×3...kiyā na koī. ...Rahama...2
Apane maśidakā zādū Gaṇū hei ...×2
Mālika hamāre ...×3...Tuma Bābā Sāī... Rahama...3

12. Janī Pada

Tuja kāya deū Sāvaḷyā mī khāyā tarī ho
Tuja kāya deū Sadguru mi khāyā tarī ho
Mī dubalī batīka Nāmyācī jāṇa Śrī Harī ...×2...dhṛ
Ucchiṣṭa tulā deṇe hī goṣṭa nā barī ho ...×2
Tū Jagannātha, tuja deu kaśire bhākarī ...×2
Nako aṅta madīya pāhū Sakhyā, Bhagavaṅtā Śrīkaṅtā
Mādhyānha rātra ulaṭoni gelī hī ātā. Āṇa cittā.
Jā hoīla tuzā re kākaḍā kī rāuḷāṅtarī ho ...×2
Ānatīla bhakta naivedyahī nānāparī ...×2...dhṛ

13. Śrī Sadguru Pada

Śrī Sadguru Bābā Sāī ho ...×2
Tuja vāṅcuni āśraya nāhī, bhūtāli ...×2...dhṛ
Mi pāpī patita dhīmaṅda ...×2
Tāraṇe malā Gurunāthā, zaḍakarī ...×2...1
Tū śānti ksmecā meru ho ...×2
Tū bhavārnavīce tārū, Guruvarā ...×2...2
Guruvarā majasi pāmarā, ātā uddharā
(tvarīta lavalāhī) ...×2
Mī buḍato bhavabhaya ḍohī ...×2
Śrī Sadguru ...3

Lalakāra

Śrī Saccidānaṁda Sadguru
Sāīnāthā Mahārāja kī Jaya
Auṁ Rājādhirāja Yogīrāja
Parabrahma Sāīnātha Mahārāja
Śrī Saccidānaṁda Sadguru
Sāīnātha Mahārāja ki Jaya

NOON ARATI AT 12.00 P.M.
MĀDHYĀNHA ĀRATĪ

---

1. Pañcāratī

Gheuniyā pañcāratī, karū Bābāṅsī āratī.
Sāīsi āratī...

[Ī. naṁ 5 pramāṇe mhaṇaṇe]

2. Āratī Sāībābā

Āratī Sāī Bābā. Saukhyadātāra jīvā.
Caraṇarajātalī
Dyāvā dāsā visāvā, bhaktāṅ visāvā. ...Ā...dhṛ
Jāḷūniyā anaṅga. Svasvarūpi rāhe daṅga
Mumukṣu janāṅ dāvī. Nija ḍoḷā Śriraṅga
Ḍoḷā Śriraṅga ...Ā...1
Jayā manī jaisā bhāva.
Tayātaisā anubhava Dāvisī dayāghanā.
Aisī [(tuzī hī māva)...×2] ...Ā...2
Tumace nāma dhyātā. Hare saṅsṛtivyathā
Agādha tava karaṇī. Marga [dāvisī anāthā) ...×2] ...Ā...3
Kaliyugī avatāra Saguṇa Brahma sācāra.
Avatīrṇa zālāse. Svāmi [Datta Digaṁbara) ...×2] ...Ā...4
Āṭhāṅ divasā guruvārī. Bhakta karitī vārī.
Prabhupada pahāvayā. Bhava [(bhaya nivārī) ...×2] ...Ā...5

Māzā nijadravya ṭhevā. Tava caraṇa-raja-sevā māgne hecī ātā.
Tumhāṅ [(Devādhi devā) ...×2] ...Ā...6
Icchita dīna cātaka. Nirmala toya nijasūkha
Pājāveṅ mādhavā yā. Sāṁbhāḷa [(āpulī bhāka) ...×2] ...Ā...7

2 A. Jaya Deva

Jaya Deva Jaya Deva Dattā Avadhūtā,
O Sāī Avadhūtā,
Joḍuni kara tava caraṇi ṭhevito māthā.
Jaya Deva, Jaya Deva. ...dhṛ
Avatarasī tū yetā dharmāte glānī nāsti kāṅ nāhi
tū lāvisī nijabhajanī
Dāvisī nānā līlā asaṅkhya rūpānī,
Harīsī dīnāṅce tū saṅkaṭa dinarajanī. ...1...Jaya...
Yavana-svarūpī ekyā darśana tvā didhale
Saṁśaya nirasuniyā tadavaitā ghālavile
Gopīcaṅdā Maṅdā tvācī uddarile
Momina vaṅśī janmuni lokāṅ tāriyale. ...2...Jaya...
Bheda na tattavī Hiṅdu-yavanāṅca kāhi
Dāvāyāsi zālā punarapi naradehī
Pāhasī premāne tū Hiṅdū-yavanāṅhī
Dāvisī ātmatvāne vȳapaka hā Sāī. ...3...Jaya...
Devā Sāīnāthā tvatpadanata vhāve
Paramāyā mohita janamocana zaṇi vhāve
Tvakṛpayā saklāṅce saṅkata nirasāve
Deśila tarī de tvadyaśa Kṛṣṇāne gāve. ...4...Jaya....

3. Śiraḍī māze Paṅḍharapura

Śiraḍī māze Paṅdḥarapura. Sāī Bābā Ramāvara.
Bābā Ramavāra. ...1...Sāī...
Śuddha bhaktī Caṅdrabhāgā. Bhāva Puṅḍalīka jāgā.
Puṅḍalīka jāgā. ...2...Bhāva...
Yā ho yā ho avaghe jana. Karā Bābāṅsī vaṅdana.
Bābāṅsī vaṅdana. ...3...Sāīsī...
Gaṇū mhaṇe Bābā Sāī. Dhāva pāva māze āī.
Pāva māze āī. ...4...Dhāva...

4. Ghālīna loṭāṅgaṇa

Ghālīna loṭāṅgaṇa vaṅdīna caraṇa,
  ḍolyāṅnī pāhīna rūpa tuze
Preme āliṅgina, ānaṅde pūjina,
  bhāve ovāḷina mhaṇe Nāmā. ...1
Tvameva mātā ca pitā tvameva,
  tvameva baṅdhuśca sakhā tvameva
Tvameva vidyā draviṇaṁ tvameva,
  tvameva sarvaṁ mama, Deva Deva. ...2
Kāyena vācā manaseṅdriyairvā,
  buddhayātmanā va prakṛti svabhāvat
Karomi yadyatsakalaṁ parasmai,
  Nārāyaṇāyeti samarpayāmi. ...3
Acyutaṁ Keśavaṁ Rāmanārāyaṇaṁ,
  Kṛṣṇadāmodaraṁ Vāsudevaṁ Harim
Śrīdharaṁ Mādhavaṁ Gopikāvallabhaṁ,
  Janakīnāyakaṁ Rāmacaṅdraṅ bhaje. ...4

5. Namasmarana

Hare Rāma, Hare Rāma, Rāma Rāma Hare Hare
Hare Kṛṣṇa, Hare Kṛṣṇa, Kṛṣṇa Kṛṣṇa Hare Hare
(Iti Trivāra)

Śrī Gurudeva Datta

6. Puṣpāñjalī

Hari Auṁ yajñena yajñamayajaṅta
devāstāni dharmāṇi prathamānyāsan
Te ha nākaṁ mahimānaḥ sacaṅta yatra
pūrve sādhyā saṅti devāḥ.
Auṁ Rājādhirājāya prasahyasāhine namo
vayam Vaiśravaṇāya kurmahe.
Sa me kāmānkāmakāmāya mahayaṁ
Kāmeśvaro Vaiśravaṇo dadhātu Kuberāya
Vaiśravaṇāya Mahārājāya namaḥ.
Auṁ Svasti. Sāmrājaṁ Bhaujyaṁ Svārājyaṁ Vairājyaṁ
Pāramesthayaṁ Rājyaṁ Māhārājyamādhipatya mayaṁ
Samantaparyāyī Syātsārvabhaumaḥ Sārvāyuṣya
Āṅtādāparārdhāt pṛthivyai samudraparyaṅtāyā ekrāḷiti.
Tadapyeṣa ślok'bhi gīto Marutaḥ
pariveṣṭāro Maruttasyāvasaṅgṛhe.
Avikṣitasya kāmparerviśvedevāḥ sabhāsada iti.
Śrī Nārāyaṇa Vāsudeva Saccidānaṅda Sadguru
Sāīnātha Mahārāja kī Jaya

7. Namaskārāṣṭaka

Anaṁtā tulā te kase re stavāve
Anaṁtā tulā te kase re namāve
Anaṁtā mukhāṅcā śine śeṣa gātāṅ
Namaskāra ṣāṣṭānga Śrī Sāīnāthā. ...1
Smarāve manī tvatpadā nitya bhāve
Urāve tarī bhaktisāṭhī svabhāve
Tarāve jagā tārūnī māyatātā. ...2...Namaskāra...
Vase jo sadā dāvayā saṁta līlā
Dise ajñya lokāṅparī jo janāṁlā
Parī aṁtarī jñāna kaivalyadātā. ...3...Namaskāra...
Barā lādhalā janma hā mānavācā
Narā sārthakā sādhanībhūta sācā
Dharu Sāī preme gaḷāyā ahaṁtā. ...4...Namaskāra...
Dharāve karī sāna ālpajña bālā
Karāve amhāṅ dhanya cuṁboni gālā
Mukhī ghālā preme kharā grāsa ātā. ...5...Namaskāra...
Surādika jyāṅcyā padā vaṁditātī
Śukādika jyāte samānatva detī
Prayāgādi tīrthe padī namra hotā. ...6...Namaskāra...
Tuzyā jyā padā pāhatā Gopabālī
Sadā raṅgalī citsvarūpī miḷālī
Karī rāsakrīḍā save Kṛṣṇanāthā. ...7...Namaskāra...
Tulā māgato māgaṇe eka dyāve
Karā joḍito dīna atyaṁta bhāve
Bhavī Mohanīrāja hā tāri ātā....8...Namaskāra...

8. Aisā yeī Bā

Aisā yeī Bā. Sāī Digaṁbarā. Akṣyarūpa avatārā,
Sarvahi vyāpaka tū. Śrutisārā. Anusayā-'Trikumārā.
...dhr...Aisā yeī Bā.
Kāśī snāna japa, pratidvaśi. Kolhāpura bhikṣesī,
Nirmala nadī Tuṅgā, jala prāśī. Nidrā Māhura deśī. ...1...Aisā...
Zoḷī loṁbatase vāma karī. Trīśūlaḍamaru-dhārī,
Bhaktāṅ vārada sadā sukhakārī. Deśīla muktī cārī. ...2...Aisā...
Pāyī pādukā japamālā kamaṅḍalu mṛgachālā,
Dhāraṇa kariśī Bā,
Nāgajaṭā muguṭa śobhato māthā. ...3...Aisā...
Tatpara tuzyā yā je dhyānī. Akṣaya tyāṅce sadanī,
Lakṣmī vāsa karī dinarajanī. Rakṣisi saṅkaṭa vāruni.
...4...Aisā...
Yā pari dhyāna tuze Gururāyā dṛśya karī nayanāṅ yā,
Pūrṇānaṅda sukhe hī kāyā.
Lāvisi Hariguṇa gāyā. ...5...Aisā...dhṛ

9. Śrī Sāīnāthā Mahimna Stotrama

Sadā satsvarūpaṁ cidānaṅda kaṅdaṁ
jagatsaṁbhavasthāna saṁhāra he tum,
Svabhaktecchayā mānusaṁ darśyaṁ taṁ
namāmiśvāraṁ Sadguruṁ Sāīnāthām. ...1
Bhavadhvāṅtavidhvaṁ sa mārtaṅḍamīḍayaṁ
manovāggatītaṁ munīrdhyānangamyam,
Jagat-vyāpakaṁ nirmalaṁ nirguṇaṁtvāṁ,
namāmī. ...2

Bhavāṁbhodhi magnārditānāṁ janānāṁ
svapādā-śrītānāṁ svabhaktipriyāṇām,
Samuddhāraṇārtha kalau saṁbhavaṅtaṁ,
namāmī. ...3
Sadā niṁbavṛksasya mūlādhivāsātsudhāstrāviṇaṁ
titkamapyapriyaṁ tam,
Taruṅ kalpavṛksādhikaṁ sādhayaṅtaṁ,
namāmī. ...4
Sadā kalpavṛkṣasya tasyadhimūle
bhavedbhāvabuddhayā Saparyādisevām
Nṛṇāṁ kurvatāṁ bhuktimukti pradaṁ taṁ,
namāmī. ...5
Anekāśrutātarkyalīlāvilāsāīḥ, samāviṣkṛteśāna
bhāsvatprabhāvam,
Ahaṁ bhāvahīnaṁ prasannātmabhāvaṁ,
namāmī. ...6
Satāṁ viśrāmārāmamevābhirāmam
sadā sajjanaiḥ
Saṅstutaṁ sannamaddhiḥ janāmodadaṁ
bhaktabhadra-pradaṁ taṁ
namāmī. ...7
Ajanmādyamekaṁ paraṁ brahma sāksātsvayaṁ
saṁbhavaṁ rāmamevāvatīrṇam,
Bhavadarśanātsaṁpunītaḥ prabho' haṁ,
namāmī. ...8
Śrī Sāīśa kṛpānidhe' khilanṛṇām sarvārthasiddhiprada,
Yuṣmatpādarajaḥ prabhāvamatulaṁ dhātāpivaktā' kṣamaḥ,
Sadbhaktyā śaraṇaṁ kṛtānjaliputaḥ saṁprāpito' smi Prabho,
Śrimat Sāī pareśapādakamalānnānyaccharaṇyaṁ mama. ...9

Sāīrūpadhara Rāghavottamaṁ
bhaktakāma-vibudhadrumaṁ Prabhum,
Māyayopahatacittaśūddhaye,
ciṁtayā myahamaharniśaṁ-mudā. ...10
Śaratsudhāü śupratima-prakāśaṁ,
kṛpātapatraṁ tava Sāīnātha,
Tvadīyapādābja samāśrītānāṁ
svacchāyayā tāpamapākarotu. ...11
Upāsanādaivata Sāīnātha,
stavairmayopāsaninā stutastvam,
Ramenmano me tava pādayugme,
bhṛṁgo, yathābje makaraṁdalubdhaḥ. ...12
Anekajanmārjitapāpasaukṣayo
bhavedbhavatpāda saroja darśanāt,
Ksamasva sarvānaparādhapūṁjakāṁprasīda
Sāīsa Guro dayānidhe. ...13
Śrī Sāīnātha caraṇāmṛta pūtacittāstatpāda
sevanaratāḥ satataṁ ca bhaktyā,
Saü sāra janya duritaudhavinirgatāste
kaivalyadhāma paramaṁ samvāpnuvanti. ...14
Stotrametatpaṭhedbhaktyā yo narastanmanāḥ sadā,
Sadguru Sāīnāthasya kṛpā pātraṁ bhaved dhruvam. ...15
Sāīnātha kṛpā sarvadrusatpadya kusumāvaliḥ,
Śreyase ca manah śudhyai premasūtreṇa guṁfitā. ...16
Goviṁdasūriputreṇa Kāśīnāthābhidhāyinā,
Upāsanītyupākhyena Śrī Sāī Gurave' rpitā. ...17
Iti Śrī Sāīnātha Mahimna Stotram saṁpūrṇam.

10. Prārthanā

Karacaraṇakṛtaṁ vākkāyajaṁ karmajaṁ vā
Śravaṇanayanajaṁ vā mānasaṁ vā' parādham,
Viditamaviditaṁ vā sarvametatkṣamasva.
Jaya jaya karunābdhe Śrī Prabho Sāīnātha

Lalakāra

Śrī Saccidānaṁda Sadguru Sāīnātha Mahārāja kī Jaya.
Auṁ Rājādhirāja Yogirāja Parabrahma Sāīnātha Mahārāja
Śrī Saccidānaṁda Sadguru Sāīnātha Mahārāja kī Jaya.

EVENING ARATI AT 6.15 P.M.
DHŪPA ĀRATĪ

1. Āratī Sāībābā

Āratī Sāī Bābā. Saukhyadātāra jīvā.
Caraṇarajātalī
Dyāvā dāsā visāvā, bhaktāṅ visāvā. ...Ā...dhṛ
Jāḷūniyā anaṅga. Svasvarūpi rāhe daṅga
Mumukṣu janāṅ dāvī. Nija ḍoḷā Śrīraṅga
Ḍoḷā Śrīraṅga ...Ā...1
Jayā manī jaisā bhāva.
Tayātaisā anubhava Dāvisī dayāghanā.
Aisī [(tuzī hī māva)...×2] ...Ā...2
Tumace nāma dhyātā. Hare saṁsṛtivyathā
Agādha tava karaṇī. Marga [dāvisī anāthā) ...×2] ...Ā...3
Kaliyugī avatāra Saguṇa Brahma sācāra.
Avatīrṇa zālāse. Svāmi [Datta Digaṁbara) ...×2] ...Ā...4
Āṭhāṅ divasā guruvārī. Bhakta karitī vārī.
Prabhupada pahāvayā. Bhava [(bhaya nivārī) ...×2] ...Ā...5
Māzā nijadravya ṭhevā. Tava caraṇa-raja-sevā māgne hecī ātā.
Tumhāṅ [(Devādhi devā) ...×2] ...Ā...6
Icchita dīna cātaka. Nirmala toya nijasūkha
Pājāveṅ mādhavā yā. Sāṁbhāḷa [(āpulī bhāka) ...×2] ...Ā...7

2. Śiraḍī māze Paṅdharapura

Śiraḍī māze Paṅdḥarapura. Sāī Bābā Ramāvara.
Bābā Ramavāra. ...1...Sāī...
Śuddha bhaktī Caṅdrabhāgā. Bhāva Puṅḍalīka jāgā.
Puṅḍalīka jāgā. ...2...Bhāva...
Yā ho yā ho avaghe jana. Karā Bābāṅsī vaṅdana.
Bābāṅsī vaṅdana. ...3...Sāīsī...
Gaṇū mhaṇe Bābā Sāī. Dhāva pāva māze āī.
Pāva māze āī. ...4...Dhāva...

3. Ghālīna loṭāṅgaṇa

Ghālīna loṭāṅgaṇa vaṅdīna caraṇa,
    ḍoḷyāṅnī pāhīna rūpa tuze
Preme āliṅgina, ānaṅde pūjina,
    bhāve ovāḷina mhaṇe Nāmā. ...1
Tvameva mātā ca pitā tvameva,
    tvameva baṅdhuśca sakhā tvameva
Tvameva vidyā draviṇaṁ tvameva,
    tvameva sarvaṁ mama, Deva Deva. ...2
Kāyena vācā manaseṅdriyairvā,
    buddhayātmanā va prakṛti svabhāvat
Karomi yadyatsakalaṁ parasmai,
    Nārāyaṇāyeti samarpayāmi. ...3
Acyutaṁ Keśavaṁ Rāmanārāyaṇaṁ,
    Kṛṣṇadāmodaraṁ Vāsudevaṁ Harim
Śrīdharaṁ Mādhavaṁ Gopikāvallabhaṁ,
    Janakīnāyakaṁ Rāmacaṅdraṅ bhaje. ...4

4. Namasmarana

Hare Rāma, Hare Rāma, Rāma Rāma Hare Hare
Hare Kṛṣṇa, Hare Kṛṣṇa, Kṛṣṇa Kṛṣṇa Hare Hare
(Iti Trivāra)

5. Namaskārāṣṭaka

Anaṅtā tulā te kase re stavāve
Anaṅtā tulā te kase re namāve
Anaṅtā mukhāṅcā śine śeṣa gātāṅ
Namaskāra ṣāṣṭānga Śrī Sāīnāthā. ...1
Smarāve manī tvatpadā nitya bhāve
Urāve tarī bhaktisāṭhī svabhāve
Tarāve jagā tārūnī māyatātā. ...2...Namaskāra...
Vase jo sadā dāvayā saṅta līlā
Dise ajñya lokāṅparī jo janāṅlā
Parī aṅtarī jñāna kaivalyadātā. ...3...Namaskāra...
Barā lādhalā janma hā mānavācā
Narā sārthakā sādhanībhūta sācā
Dharu Sāī preme gaḷāyā ahaṅtā. ...4...Namaskāra...
Dharāve karī sāna ālpajña bālā
Karāve amhāṅ dhanya cuṁboni gālā
Mukhī ghālā preme kharā grāsa ātā. ...5...Namaskāra...
Surādīka jyāṅcyā padā vaṅditātī
Śukādīka jyāte samānatva detī
Prayāgādi tīrthe padī namra hotā. ...6...Namaskāra...
Tuzyā jyā padā pāhatā Gopabālī
Sadā raṅgalī citsvarūpī miḷālī
Karī rāsakrīḍā save Kṛṣṇanāthā. ...7...Namaskāra...

Tulā māgato māgaṇe eka dyāve
Karā joḍito dīna atyaṅta bhāve
Bhavī Mohanīrāja hā tāri ātā....8...Namaskāra...

6. Aisā yeī Bā

Aisā yeī Bā. Sāī Digaṁbarā. Akṣyarūpa avatārā,
Sarvahi vyāpaka tū. Śrutisārā. Anusayā-'Trikumārā.
...dhr...Aisā yeī Bā.
Kāśī snāna japa, pratidvaśi. Kolhāpura bhikṣesī,
Nirmala nadī Tuṅgā, jala prāśī. Nidrā Māhura deśī. ...1...Aisā...
Zoḷī loṁbatase vāma karī. Triśūladamaru-dhārī,
Bhaktāṅ vārada sadā sukhakārī. Deśila muktī cārī. ...2...Aisā...
Pāyī pādukā japamālā kamaṅḍalu mṛgachālā,
Dhāraṇa kariśī Bā,
Nāgajaṭā muguṭa śobhato māthā. ...3...Aisā...
Tatpara tuzyā yā je dhyānī. Akṣaya tyāṅce sadanī,
Lakṣmī vāsa karī dinarajanī. Rakṣisi saṅkaṭa vāruni.
...4...Aisā...
Yā pari dhyāna tuze Gururāyā dṛśya karī nayanāṅ yā,
Pūrṇānaṅda sukhe hī kāyā.
Lāvisi Hariguṇa gāyā. ...5...Aisā...dhṛ

7. Śrī Sāīnāthā Mahimna Stotrama

Sadā satsvarūpaṁ cidānaṅda kaṅdaṁ
jagatsaṁbhavasthāna saṁhāra he tum,
Svabhaktecchayā mānusaṁ darśyaṁ taṁ
namāmiśvāraṁ Sadguruṁ Sāīnāthām. ...1

Bhavadhvāṅtavidhvaù sa mārtaṅḍamīḍayaṁ
manovāggatītaṁ munīrdhyānangamyam,
Jagat-vyāpakaṁ nirmalaṁ nirguṇaṁtvāṁ,
namāmī. ...2
Bhavāṁbhodhi magnārditānāṁ janānāṁ
svapādā-śrītānāṁ svabhaktipriyāṇām,
Samuddhāraṇārtha kalau saṁbhavaṅtaṁ,
namāmī. ...3
Sadā niṁbavṛksasya mūlādhivāsātsudhāstrāviṇaṁ
titkamapyapriyaṁ tam,
Taruṅ kalpavṛkṣādhikaṁ sādhayaṅtaṁ,
namāmī. ...4
Sadā kalpavṛkṣasya tasyadhimūle
bhavedbhāvabuddhayā Saparyādisevām
Nṛṇāṁ kurvatāṁ bhuktimukti pradaṁ taṁ,
namāmī. ...5
Anekāśrutātarkyalīlāvilāsaīḥ, samāviṣkṛteśāna
bhāsvatprabhāvam,
Ahaṁ bhāvahīnaṁ prasannātmabhāvaṁ,
namāmī. ...6
Satāṁ viśrāmārāmamevābhirāmam
sadā sajjanaiḥ
Saṅstutaṁ sannamaddhiḥ janāmodadaṁ
bhaktabhadra-pradaṁ taṁ
namāmī. ...7
Ajanmādyamekaṁ paraṁ brahma sāksātsvayaṁ
saṁ bhavaṁ rāmamevāvatīrṇam,
Bhavadarśanātsaṁ punītaḥ prabho' haṁ,
namāmī. ...8

Śrī Sāīśa kṛpānidhe' khilanṛṇām sarvārthasiddhiprada,
Yuṣmatpādarajaḥ prabhāvamatulaṁ dhātāpivaktā' kṣamaḥ,
Sadbhaktyā śaraṇaṁ kṛtānjaliputaḥ saṁ prāpito' smi Prabho,
Śrimat Sāī pareśapādakamalānnānyaccharaṇyaṁ mama. ...9
Sāīrūpadhara Rāghavottamaṁ
bhaktakāma-vibudhadrumaṁ Prabhum,
Māyayopahatacittaśūddhaye,
ciṅtayā myahamaharniśaṁ-mudā. ...10
Śaratsudhāū śupratima-prakāśaṁ,
kṛpātapatraṁ tava Sāīnātha,
Tvadīyapādābja samāśrītānāṁ
svacchāyayā tāpamapākarotu. ...11
Upāsanādaivata Sāīnātha,
stavairmayopāsaninā stutastvam,
Ramenmano me tava pādayugme,
bhṛṅgo, yathābje makaraṅdalubdhaḥ. ...12
Anekajanmārjitapāpasaukṣayo
bhavedbhavatpāda saroja darśanāt,
Ksamasva sarvānaparādhapūṅjakāṅprasīda
Sāīsa Guro dayānidhe. ...13
Śrī Sāīnātha caraṇāmṛta pūtacittāstatpāda
sevanaratāḥ satataṁ ca bhaktyā,
Saṁ sāra janya duritaudhavinirgatāste
kaivalyadhāma paramaṁ samvāpnuvanti. ...14
Stotrametatpaṭhedbhaktyā yo narastanmanāḥ sadā,
Sadguru Sāīnāthasya kṛpā pātraṁ bhaved dhruvam. ...15
Sāīnātha kṛpā sarvadrusatpadya kusumāvaliḥ,
Śreyase ca manah śudhyai premasūtreṇa guṁfitā. ...16

Govindasūriputreṇa Kāśīnāthābhidhāyinā,
Upāsanityupākhyena Śrī Sāī Gurave' rpitā. ...17
Iti Śrī Sāīnātha Mahimna Stotram saṁpūrṇam.

8. Śrī Guruprasāda - Yācanā - Daśata

Ruso mama priyāṁbikā majavarī pitāhī ruso,
Ruso mama priyaṅganā, priyasutātmajāhī ruso.
Ruso bhagini baṅdhuhī, śvaśura sāsubāī ruso,
Na Datta Guru Sāī mā, majavarī kadhīhī ruso. ...1
Puso na sūnabaī tyā maja na bhrātṛjāyā puso
Puso na priya soyare, priya sage na jñātī puso.
Puso suhṛda nā sakhā, svajana nāptabaṅdhū puso,
Parī na Guru Sāī mā, majavarī kadhīhi ruso. ...2
Puso na abalā mule, taruṇa vṛddhaī nā puso,
Puso na Guru dhākute, maja na thora sāne puso.
Puso naca bhalebure, sujana sādhuhī nā puso,
Parī na Guru Sāī mā, majavarī kadhīhī ruso. ...3
Ruso catura tattavavit vibudha prājña jñānī ruso,
Rusohī viduṣī striyā kuśala paṅḍitāhī ruso.
Ruso mahipatī yatī bhajaka tāpasīhī ruso,
Na Datta Guru Sāī mā, majavarī kadhīhī ruso. ...4
Ruso kavi ṛṣī munī anagha siddha yogī ruso,
Ruso hi gṛhadevatā, ni kulagrāmadevī ruso.
Ruso khala piśāccahī malina ḍākinīhī ruso,
Na Datta Guru Sāī mā majavarī kadhīhī ruso. ...5
Ruso mṛga khaga kṛmī, akhila jivajaṅtū ruso,
Ruso viṭapa prastarā acala āpagābdhī ruso.
Ruso kha pavanāgni vāra avani pañcatattve ruso,
Na Datta Guru Sāī mā, majavarī kadhīhi ruso. ...6

Ruso vimala kinnarā amala yakṣiṇīhī ruso,
Ruso śaśi khagādihī, gagani tārakāhī ruso.
Ruso amararājahī adaya Dharmarājā ruso,
Na Datta Guru Sāī mā, majavarī kadhīhi ruso. ...7
Ruso mana sarasvatī, capalacitta tehī ruso,
Ruso vapu diśakhila kaṭhiṇa kāla tohī ruso.
Ruso sakala viśvahī mayi tu brahmagola ruso,
Na Datta Guru Sāī mā, majavarī kadhīhi ruso. ...8
Vimūḍha mhaṇūni haso, maja na matsarāhī ḍaso,
Padābhirūci ulhaso, jananakardamī nā faso.
Na durga dhṛticā dhaso, aśivabhāva māge khaso,
Prapañci mana he ruso, dṛḍha virakti citti ṭhaso. ...9
Kuṇācihi ghṛṇā naso na ca spṛhā kaśācī aso,
Sadaiva hṛdayī vaso, manasi dhyāni Sāī vaso.
Padī praṇaya vorso, nikhila dṛśya Bābā diso,
Na Datta Guru Sāī mā, upari yācanelā ruso. ...10

9. Puspāñjalī

Hari Auṁ yajñena yajñamayajaṅta
devāstāni dharmāṇi prathamānyāsan
Te ha nākaṁ mahimānaḥ sacaṅta yatra
pūrve sādhyā saṅti devāḥ.
Auṁ Rājādhirājāya prasahyasāhine namo
vayam Vaiśravaṇāya kurmahe.
Sa me kāmānkāmakāmāya mahayaṁ
Kāmeśvaro Vaiśravaṇo dadhātu Kuberāya
Vaiśravaṇāya Mahārājāya namaḥ.

Aum̐ Svasti. Sāmrājam̐ Bhaujyam̐ Svārājyam̐ Vairājyam̐
Pāramesthayam̐ Rājyam̐ Māhārājyamādhipatya mayam̐
Samantaparyāyī Syātsārvabhaumaḥ Sārvāyuṣya
Āṅtādāparārdhāt pṛthivyai samudraparyaṅtāyā ekrāḷiti.
Tadapyeṣa ślok'bhi gīto Marutaḥ
pariveṣṭāro Maruttasyāvasaṅgṛhe.
Avikṣitasya kāmparerviśvedevāḥ sabhāsada iti.
Śrī Nārāyaṇa Vāsudeva Saccidānaṅda Sadguru
Sāīnātha Mahārāja kī Jaya

10. Prārthanā

Karacaraṇakṛtam̐ vākkāyajam̐ karmajam̐ vā
Śravaṇanayanajam̐ vā mānasam̐ vā' parādham,
Viditamaviditam̐ vā sarvametatkṣamasva.
Jaya jaya karunābdhe Śrī Prabho Sāīnātha

Lalakāra

Śrī Saccidānaṅda Sadguru Sāīnātha Mahārāja kī Jaya.
Aum̐ Rājādhirāja Yogirāja Parabrahma Sāīnātha Mahārāja
Śrī Saccidānaṅda Sadguru Sāīnātha Mahārāja kī Jaya.

NIGHT ARATI AT 10.00 P.M.
ŚEJA ĀRATĪ

1. Pāñcāhī Tattvañcī Āratī

Ovāḷū āratī māzyā Sagurunāthā, māzyā Sāīnāthā,
Pāñcāhī tatvāñcā dīpa lāvilā ātā ...dhṛ
Nirguṇācī sthiti keisī ākārā ālī, Bābā ākārā ālī,
Sarvā ghaṭī bharūni uralī Sāī māulī. ...1...Ovāḷū...dhṛ
Raja tama sattva tighe māyā prasavalī,
mazyāvāra māyā prasavalī
Māyāciye poṭī keisī māyā udbhavalī. ...2...Ovāḷū....dhṛ
Saptasāgarī keisā kheḷa māṅḍīlā, Bābā kheḷa māṅḍilā,
Kheḷūniyā kheḷa avaghā vistāra kelā. ...3...Ovāḷū...dhṛ...
Brahmāṅḍīcī racanā keisī dākhavilī ḍoḷā, Bābā dākhavilī ḍoḷā,
Tukā mhaṇe māzā Svāmī kṛpāḷū bhoḷā. ...4...Ovāḷū...dhṛ...

2. Āratī Jñānarāyācī

Āratī Jñānarājā. Māhākeivalyatejā,
Sevitī sādhu santa. Manu vedhalā māzā.
Āratī Jñānarājā. ...dhṛ
Lopale jñāna jagī. Hita neṇatī koṇī,
Avatāra Pāṅḍuraṅga. Nāma ṭhevīle jñāni. ...1...Āratī...
Kanakāce tāṭa karī. Ubhyā Gopikā nārī,
Nārada Tuṁbaraho. Sāmagāyana karī. ...2...Āratī...

Pragaṭa guhya bole. Viśva Brahmaci kele,

Rāma Janārdanī. Pāyī mastaka ṭhevile. ...3...Āratī...

3. Āratī Tukārāmācī

Āratī Tukārāmā. Svāmī Sadgurudhāmā,

Saccidānaṁda mūrtī. Pāya dākhavī āmhāṁ.

Āratī Tukārāmā. ...dhṛ

Rāghave sāgarāta. Jaise pāṣāṇa tārile,

Teise he Tukobāce. Abhaṁga rakṣile. ...1...dhṛ

Tukitā tulanesi, Brahma Tukāsī āle,

Mhaṇonī Rameśvare, caraṇī mastaka ṭhevile ...2...dhṛ

4. Jaya Jaya Sāīnātha

Jaya jaya Sāīnātha ātā pahuḍāve maṁdirī ho, ...×2

Aḷavito sapreme tujalā āratī gheuni karī ho.

Jaya jaya Sāīnātha ātā pahuḍāve maṁdirī ho. ...dhṛ

Raṁjavisī tū madhura bolunī māya jaśī nija mulā ho ...×2

Bhogisi vyādhī tūca haruniyā nija sevaka duhkhālā ho ...×2

Dhāvuni bhakta vyasana harisī darśana desī tyālā ho ...×2

Zāle asatila kaṣṭa atīśaya tumace yā dehālā ho.

...1...Jaya...dhṛ...

Kṣamā śayana suṁdara hī śobhā sumana śeja tyāvarī ho ...×2

Ghyāvī thoḍī bhakta janāṁcī pūjanādi cākarī ho. ...×2

Ovāḷito pañcaprāṇa jyoti sumatī karī ho. ...×2

Sevā kiṁkara bhakta prīti attara parimaḷa vārī ho.

...2...Jaya...dhṛ...

Soḍuni jāyā duḥkha vāṭate Sāī tvaccaraṇāṅsī ho ...×2
Ājñestava tava āśīprasāda gheuni nija sadanāsī ho ...×2
Jāto ātā yeū punarapi tvaccaraṇāce pāsī ho ...×2
Uṭhavū tujalā Sāīmāule nijahita sādhāyāsī ho. ...3...Jaya...dhṛ...

5. Ātā Svāmi Sukhe

Ātā Svāmī sukhe nidrā karā Avadhūtā.
Bābā karā, Sāīnāthā,
Cinmaya he sukhadhāmā jāuni pahuḍā ekāṅtā ...dhṛ
Vairāgyācā kuṅcā gheuni cauka zāḍīlā. Bābā cauka zāḍīlā.
Tyāvarī supremācā śiḍakāvā didhalā. ...1...Ātā...dhṛ
Pāyaghaḍayā ghātalyā sundara navavidhā bhakti
Bābā navavidhā bhakti,
Jñānācyā samayā lāvuni ujaḷayā jyotī. ...2...Ātā...dhṛ...
Bhāvārthācā maṅcaka hṛdayākāśī ṭāṅgilā. Bābā kāśī ṭāṅgilā,
Manācī sumane karunī kele śejelā. ...3...Ātā...dhṛ...
Dvaitāce kapāṭa lāvuni ekatra kele. Bābā ekatra kele,
Durbuddicyā gāṭhi soḍūni paḍade soḍile. ...4...Ātā...dhṛ...
Āsā tṛṣṇā kalpaneca soḍūni galabalā. Bābā soḍūni galabalā,
Dayā kṣamā śāṅti dāsī ubhyā sevelā. ...5...Ātā...dhṛ...
Alakṣya unmanī gheunī Bābā nājuka duḥśālā
Bābā nājuka duḥśālā,
Nirañjana Sadguru Svāmī nijavile śejelā. ...6...Ātā...dhṛ...
Sadguru Sāīnātha Mahārāja kī Jaya.
Śrī Gurudeva Datta.

6. Prasāda Miḷaṇyākaritā (Abhaṅga)

Pāhe prasādācī vāṭa. Dyāve dhuvoniyā tāṭa. ...1

Śeṣa gheunī jāīna. Tumace zāliyā bhojana. ...2

Zālo ātā ekasevā. Tumhā āḷavito Devā. ...3

Tukā mhaṇe ātā citta. Karuni rāhilo niścita. ...4

7. Prasāda Milāḷyānaṅtara (Pada)

Pāvalā prasāda ātā Vitho nijāve. Bābā ātā nijāve,
Āpulā to śrama kaḷo yetase bhāve. ...1
Ātā Svāmī sukhe nidrā karā Gopāḷā. Bābā Sāī dayaḷā,
Purale manoratha jāto āpule sthaḷā. ...2
Tumhāṅsī jāgavū āmhī āpulyā cāḍā. Bābā āpulyā cāḍā.
Śubhāśubha karme doṣa harāvayā pīḍā. ...3...Ātā Svāmī...
Tukā mhaṇe didhale ucchiṣṭāce bhojana. Ucchiṣṭāce bhojana,
Nāhī nivaḍile āmhāṅ āpulyā bhinna. ...4...Ātā Svāmī...

Lalakāra

Śrī Saccidānaṅda Sadguru Sāīnātha Mahārāja kī Jaya.
Auṁ Rājādhirāja Yogirāja Parabrahma Sāīnātha Mahārāja
Śrī Saccidānaṅda Sadguru Sāīnātha Mahārāja ki Jaya

8. Kṛpā Gururāja

Sāīnātha Mahārāja. Ātā kṛpā karā Gururāja. ...dhṛ
Trividhatāpa hā pāṭhi lāgalā. Kāhī na suce kāja ...1...ā
Manovṛtti hyā kitītari usaḷatī. Utarī yāṅcā māja. ...2...ā
Harisī jaisā dīna janāce. Vyasana kasunī māja. ...3...ā
Kṛṣṇadāsa tvaccaraṇī žalā. Līna tyajuni janalāja. ...4...ā

Upasaṃhāraḥ
Mānasa Bodha

Kyā kiyā mana Śiraḍī ākara Sāīnātha nā cīnāre ...dhṛ
Desa desa ghuma Śiraḍī āyā Sāī darśana līyāre
Khāyā pīyā sukhase soyā vicāra nā kachu kiyāre ...1...kyā
Auṭa hāta piṭha maṁdira suṁdara thāṭamāṭa saba dekhāre.
Jñāna nayanase Sāīnātha hṛnmaṁdira ko nā nirakhāre. ...2...kyā
Bhāta bhātake fale-mevā aru śakkara dilabhara bhākhāre
Jyo na tune Śrī Sāīnātha mukha svaprema vacana rasa cākhāre
...3...kyā
Thāṭamāṭase pūjana kara dhana māngā utanā dīyāre
Nādeke saprema bhāva ko fira fira fira pachatāyāre. ...4...kyā
Dinabharrā khuba sevā kīnī auṭa pīṭha lapaṭāyāre
Auṭa piṭha dhani lapaṭana khātira kāmakopa na khoyāre
...5...kyā
Sāī na Hiṁdu Yavana, jaba mānā sukhacaraṇaudaka pāyāre
Pācheke avatāra caritakā khopajuṁ dilabica lāyāre ...6...kyā
Dhana daulata aru maṁdira māḍī chāṁda joga jada liyāre
Tanaka tanaka be kāma kāmase rūṭha jogabala khoyāre.
...7...kyā
Sāīnātha mā tāta gusāī jāna māna saba tajanāre
Vohī Rāma aru Kṛṣṇa bharā hai saba ghaṭaghaṭa nā jānāre.
...8...kyā

Anaṁta koṭi Brahmāṁda Nāyaka
Rājādhirāja Yogīrāja Parabrahma
Śrī Saccidānaṁda Sadguru
Sāīnāthā Mahārāja ki Jaya.

Śrī Gurudeva Mahārāja ki Jaya.

SHRI SAI BABA ARCHANA (108 NAMES)

1. Om Sri Sai Nathaaya namaha
2. Om Lakshminaarayanaya namaha
3. Om Krishna Ramashiva Maruthyaadhi Roopaaya namaha
4. Om Seshasai ne namaha
5. Om Godavarithata Shirdivasi ne namaha
6. Om Bhakta Hrudaalayaaya namha
7. Om Sarva Hrunnilayyaya namaha
8. Om Bhoota Vaasaya namaha
9. Om Bhoothabhavishyadbhaava Varjnithaaya namaha
10. Om Kaalaathiithaaya namaha
11. Om Kaalaaya namaha
12. Om Kaala Kaalaaya namaha
13. Om Kaaladarpa Damanaaya namaha
14. Om Mrutyunjayaaya namaha
15. Om Amarthyaaya namaha
16. Om Marthyaabhayapradhaaya namaha
17. Om Jiivadhaaraaya namaha
18. Om Sarvadhaaraaya namaha
19. Om Bhaktaavana Samarthaaya namaha
20. Om Bhaktavana Prathikjnaaya namaha
21. Om Anna Vastra Daaya namaha
22. Om Arogya Ksheemadaaya namaha
23. Om Dhana Maangalyapradaaya namaha
24. Om Buddhi Siddhi Pradaaya namaha
25. Om Putra Mitra Kalathra Bandhudaaya namaha
26. Om Yogakshema Vahaaya namaha

27. Om Aapadbhaandhavaaya namaha
28. Om Maargabandhave namaha
29. Om Bhukti Mukti Swargaapavargadaaya namaha
30. Om Priyaaya namaha
31. Om Preeti Vardhanaaya namaha
32. Om Antharyamine namaha
33. Om Sacchitatmane namaha
34. Om Nityanandaaya namaha
35. Om Parama Sukhadaaya namaha
36. Om Parameshwaraaya namaha
37. Om Parabrahmane namaha
38. Om Paramaatmane namaha
39. Om Gnaana Swaroopine namaha
40. Om Jagath Pithre namaha
41. Om Bhaktaanaam Mathru Dhathru Pithaamahaaya namaha
42. Om Bhakta Abhaya Pradhaaya namaha
43. Om Bhakta Paradheenaya namaha
44. Om Bhaktaanugraha Karaaya namaha
45. Om Sharaanagatha Vatsalaaya namaha
46. Om Bhakti Shakti Pradaaya namaha
47. Om Gnana Vairaagya Prdaaya namaha
48. Om Prema Pradaaya namaha
49. Om Samkshaya Hrudaya Dowurbalya Papa Karma Vaasana Kshayakaraaya namaha
50. Om Hrudayagranthi Bhedakaaya namaha
51. Om Karma Dhvamsiinee namaha
52. Om Sudhasathvasthithaaya namaha
53. Om Gunaatheetha Gunaathmane namaha
54. Om Anantha Kalyaana Gunaaya namaha
55. Om Amitha Parakramaaya namaha
56. Om Jayine namaha

57. Om Durdhaarshaa Kshobyaaya namaha
58. Om Aparaajitaya namaha
59. Om Trilokeshu Avighatha Gataye namaha
60. Om Ashakya Rahitaaya namaha
61. Om Sarva Shakti Murthayee namaha
62. Om Suroopa Sundaraaya namaha
63. Om Sulochanaaya namaha
64. Om Bahuroopa Vishwamurthaye namaha
65. Om Aroopaavyaktaaya namaha
66. Om Achintyaaya namaha
67. Om Sookshmaaya namaha
68. Om Sarvaantharyamine namaha
69. Om Manovaaga Theethaya namaha
70. Om Premamoorthayee namaha
71. Om Sulabaha Durlabhaaya namaha
72. Om Asahaaya Sahaayaaya namaha
73. Om Anaatha Naatha Deenabaanhave namaha
74. Om Sarvabhaara Bhrute namaha
75. Om Akarmaaneka Karma Sukarmine namaha
76. Om Punyasravana Keerthanaaya namaha
77. Om Theerthaaya namaha
78. Om Vasudevaya namaha
79. Om Sataamgathaye namaha
80. Om Satparaynayana namaha
81. Om Lokanaathaaya namah
82. Om Paavananaaghaaya namaha
83. Om Amruthamsave namaha
84. Om Bhaskara Prabhavaya namaha
85. Om Bramhacharya Tapascharyaadi Suvrathaaya namaha
86. Om Satyadharma Paraayanaaya namaha
87. Om Siddheshvaraaya namaha
88. Om Siddha Sankalpaaya namaha

89. Om Yogeshwaraaya namaha
90. Om Bhagwate namaha
91. Om Bhakta Vatsalaaya namaha
92. Om Sathpurushaaya namaha
93. Om Purushotthamaaya namaha
94. Om Satyatatva Bodhakaaya namaha
95. Om Kaamaadi Shadvairi Dwamsine namaha
96. Om Abhedaanandaanubhava Pradhaaya namaha
97. Om Samasarvamatha Sammataaya namaha
98. Om Sri Dakshinaa Moorthiye namaha
99. Om Sri Venkatesha Ramanaaya namaha
100. Om Adbhuthaanantha Charyaaya namaha
101. Om Prapannarthi Haraaya namaha
102. Om Samsaara Sarva Dukha Kshayakaraaya namaha
103. Om Sarva Vitsarvato Mukhaaya namaha
104. Om Sarvaantharbhahi Stitaaya namaha
105. Om Sarvamangala Karaaya namaha
106. Om Sarvaabhiishta Pradhaaya namaha
107. Om Samaras Sanmaarga Sthaapanaaya namaha
108. Om Samartha Sadguru Sri Sai Nathaaya namaha

A NOTE ON THE TRANSLITERATION

The transliteration of Marathi and Sanskrit in this book is what is used internationally by students of this language. It is not an exact phonetic transcription but it can easily be used as such, as the script of this language, the Devanagari script, corresponds very regularly to the sounds.

Phonetic Alphabet or Transliteration Code

अ *a*, आ *ā*, इ *i*, ई *ī*, उ *u*, ऊ *ū*, ऋ *ṛ*, ॠ *ṝ*

ए *e*, **ऐ** *ai*, **ओ** *o*, **औ** *ou*, **अं** *ṁ*, ऽः *ḥ*,

क् *k*, **ख्** *kh*, **ग्** *g*, **घ्** *gh*, **ङ** *ṅ*,

च् *c*, **छ्** *ch*, **ज्** *j*, झ् *jh*, ञं *ñ*

ट् *ṭ*, **ठ्** *ṭh*, **ड्** *ḍ*, **ढ्** *ḍh*, **ण्** *ṇ*,

त् *t*, **थ्** *th*, **द्** *d*, **ध्** *dh*, **न** *n*,

प् *p*, **फ्** *ph*, **ब्** *b*, **भ्** *bh*, **म्** m,

य् y, र् *r*, ल् *l*, **व्** *v*,

श् *ś*, **ष्** *ṣ*, **स्** *s*, **ह्** *h*,

क्ष् *kṣ*, त्र् *tr*, **ज्ञ्** *jñ*

Vowels:

Vowels are short or long. Long vowels are indicated by a dash above. The first eight are pure vowels, as in French or Italian, and the next two are diphthongs. The English equivalents are therefore only approximate.

a as in b*u*t, c*u*p;

ā as in c*a*lm, f*a*ther;

i as in b*i*t, s*i*t;

ī as in s*ee*n, m*ea*n;

u as in p*u*t, f*oo*t

ū as in r*oo*m, m*oo*d;

e as in French l*e*s;

o as in French b*eau*;

ai a diphthong, as in hay, m*ai*ze;

au a diphthong, as in b*ou*gh, n*o*w;

ṛ is a vowel and pronounced like a rolled r;

the tilde, ~ , over a vowel indicates that it should be pronounced nasally.

Consonants:

c as reach, church;

t, *d*, and *n* are pronounced with the tip of the tongue against the top teeth as in French;

ṭ, ḍ, and ṇ are pronounced with the tip of the tongue bent back to touch the roof of the mouth;

ś an s ṣ as in s*h*ine, s*h*ower;

ñ as in o*ni*on. Spanish señor;

The sound of *jñ* is d*ny*a or g*ny*a.

When consonants are followed by *h*, they should be pronounced with a strong puff of air.

ḥ when at the end of a line indicates that the previous vowel is echoed;

when followed by *p* or *ph* is pronounced as a soft *f*;

when followed by *k* or *kh* is pronounced gutturally. as in the Scots l*oc*h;

when followed by *ś*, or *ṣ* is pronounced *ś*, *ṣ* or *s* respectively.

WITH ALL REVERENCE

Sterling Publishers have the proud privilege of releasing this unique, comprehensive and illustrative version of the Sai Satcharita by Prof. Dr. B.H. Briz-Kishore, originally written by Sri Hemadpant. Although many versions are available, this book strikingly demonstrates eternal truths to readers of all ages, vibrates their thoughts and evokes their fine feelings in realising the metaphysical manifestation of Divine power in our great Vedic land.

With all humility and reverence we wish to express our gratitude to Prof. Dr. B.H. Briz-Kishore for his valuable contribution to the progress of society. He is a versatile personality, an embodiment of integrated knowledge, an eminent educationist and an outstanding academician, besides being a scientist par excellence.

Prof. Dr. B.H. Briz-Kishore has not only been the guiding spirit behind Sterling Publishers, but is the essence of our progress and success, deeply enmeshed in every sphere of our organisation, leading us from strength to strength to achieve our ultimate goal.

S.K. Ghai

Chairman
Sterling Publishers